World War One –

The Unheard Stories of Soldiers on the Western Front Battlefields

First World War stories as told by those who fought in WW1 battles

Volume Two

Published by Triangle Circle Square Press © 2016

ISBN-13: 978-1-387-81869-3

All rights reserved. No text of this publication may be reproduced, distributed, or transmitted in any form or by any means, including photocopying, recording, or other electronic or mechanical methods, without the prior written permission of the publisher, except in the case of brief quotations embodied in critical reviews and certain other non-commercial uses permitted by copyright law.

This book features the work of several independent, private photographers. Where appropriate, they have been attributed for their work. Images used under any Creative Commons and GNU free license remain under their respective licenses.

Contents

Preface v
Original Introduction ix
Chapter I - Mons and the Great Retreat 10
Chapter II – German Atrocities 21
Chapter III - "Greenjackets" in the Firing Line 29
Chapter IV - The Struggle on the Aisne 37
Chapter V – "The Most Critical Day of All" 45
Chapter VI - British Fighters in French Wars 55
Chapter VII – German Treachery and Hatred 64
Chapter VIII – Life in the Trenches 72
Chapter IX – Sapping and Mining: The "Lucky Company" ... 81
Chapter X - L Battery's Heroic Last Stand 88
Chapter XI - A Daisy-Chain of Bandoliers 99
Chapter XII – Despatch-Riding 107

"Another battery of horse gunners was dashing to the rescue."

Preface

This collection of soldier's stories relays sobering accounts of combat on the Western Front, dating to the early stages of the First World War. Evocative descriptions of the opening months of the conflict populate these pages, from which the reader can gain lessons of both the conditions of the stagnant front, and of the message the government wished to present to the public in allowing this anthology of anecdotes to be published.

A re-enactment of WW1 prisoner taking at Fort Lytton, Brisbane, Australia - Image: David Jackmanson

We see here accounts dating from the opening months of the First World War, a conflict which from our vantage point in the 21st century is synonymous with senseless carnage, catastrophic foreign policy and consequent loss of life. They are fresh recollections made weeks or months after their occurrence; their tellers not yet worn down and still committed against the enemy, whom – we are frequently reminded – has committed many atrocities, dishonouring the battlefields and war. Horses – which were to gradually disappear as the war progressed- make frequent appearances. Initial early victories, whose promise would fast diminish in the face of stagnancy on the front, also feature.

Originally released in 1915, the set of tales within this book offer a sobering account from various battlefields which took place during the early stages of the war. Although the war was not even halfway over by the time of these stories finding publication, the horrors of the war were already a fact of life, with casualties mounting rapidly on both sides.

A recreated network of WW1 trenches at the Apedale Valley Light Railway - Image: Chris Allen

The propagandists and censors of the time allowed publication of these surprisingly frank and accurate stories for two reasons: that the German enemy was duly vilified, and that the belief in the essential victory was expressed in most of the anecdotes. Despite the horrors of war, the purpose of it was alive and its soldiers were still determined and convinced of victory. Many of the storytellers were indeed, during these early stages and victories, still assured that the Germans were monstrous and their defeat impending. The short passages preluding each story often comment pointedly about the courage, bravery and cheerfulness of the teller. Compliments by the storytellers toward their commanding officers are common.

The Coltman Trench at Staffordshire Regiment Museum is a common scene for renactments - Image: WarMagician

In 1915 public opinion hadn't yet fully turned against the war, and in Britain – the nationality of all the soldiers here – the need for showing progress was essential to sustain civilian and military morale. All of the soldiers in these pages were already serving in their regiments, or had volunteered for service, when the war commenced. They were more often professional soldiers, possessed of a natural – even ingrained - patriotism, and more accepting of the official narrative than the increasingly sceptical and fearful citizenry back home. There is however no doubt that many were already disillusioned, and that the stories here are taken from an already thinning group of soldiers still possessed of some shred of belief in the war as a noble, even glorious, conflict.

Despite the mood which underpins the pages here, one can read between the lines for a picture. The stories are honest: thing got worse between those elated first weeks wherein the French welcomed their allies so gladly, and the war that was to be over by Christmas 1914 was nowhere near ending, and it is in these stories that we witness the germinal seeds of disillusion and hatred of conflict. The majority of the illustrations which originally accompanied these accounts prioritise the heroism of their subjects, while a few offer a toned down presentation of the horrific battlefields.

The modern remnants of a World War I training trench at Bodelwyddan Castle - Image: Jeff Buck

Unheard in the modern day, it is by reading between the lines of nationalist sentiment that the truth of the front emerges. It is clear that conditions rapidly worsened as the countryside was torn asunder by conflict, and that the forces of both sides were dug in with shifts in the lines increasingly rare. The implications of this – that death and carnage would carry on for a long time – gradually hit home. However it would – thanks to the efforts of Britain's censors - take longer before the rawest accounts, stripped of all nationalism, would be published.

A World War One propaganda poster from 1915

Inevitably, the truth came out, but only after the violence had claimed an enormous and notorious toll. By word of mouth rather than the popular media of the time was the grisly truth expressed - by 1916, the rate of able volunteers had fallen such that conscription was introduced. The new depths plumbed by weapons such as poisonous gas would further drive sentiment against the war. However it was only the arrival of fresh forces from the USA in 1917, together with new technologies such as the tank replacing the woefully obsolete horse, which resulted in enough breakthrough to force the end of the horrific conflict in 1918.

In this modern edition, we include a number of relevant photographic illustrations alongside the original drawings which accompanied the stories when they were first published. While the imagery of World War I is generally quite ingrained in our minds, these supplementary pictures are designed as on-the-spot reminders of how war was more than a century ago, as well as to provide demonstration of the weapons and technology of the era.

Original Introduction

By Walter Wood, 1915

All the stories in this volume are told by men who were seen personally, and who, with one or two exceptions—cases of soldiers who had returned to the front—read the typescripts of their narratives, so that accuracy should be secured. The narrators spoke while the impressions of fighting and hardships and things seen were still strong and clear; in several cases full notes had been made or diaries kept, and reference to these records was of great value in preparing the stories. When seeing an informant I specially asked that a true tale should be told, and I believe that no unreliable details were knowingly given.

I have been fortunate in getting a good deal of exclusive matter—the full record of the noble achievement of L Battery, Royal Horse Artillery, for example, has not been given anywhere in such detail as is presented here, and the same remark applies to the story of the three torpedoed cruisers.

During the earlier periods of the war British soldiers told me tales of barbarities and outrages committed by German troops which were so terrible that it was impossible to believe them, and I omitted many of these details from the finished stories; but I know now, from reading the Report of the Committee on Alleged German Outrages, presided over by Viscount Bryce, formerly British Ambassador at Washington, that even the most dreadful of the statements did not do more than touch the fringe of the appalling truth.

Though much has been already published in the form of tales and letters from our soldiers at the front, yet I hope that this collection of stories will be accepted as a contribution from the British fighting man to the general history of the earlier stages of the war—those memorable preliminary operations which have made a deep and indelible impression on the British race throughout the world

Chapter I - Mons and the Great Retreat

Pvt J. Parkinson – Gordon Highlanders, 1st Battalion

[History does not give a more splendid story of courage and endurance than that which is afforded by the battle of Mons and the subsequent retreat. The British Expeditionary Force, straight from home, with no time for preparation, and only two days after a concentration by rail, was confronted by at least four times its number of the finest troops of Germany, and, after a four days' furious battle, remained unconquered and undismayed. What might have been annihilation of the British forces had become a throwing off of the weight of the enemy's pursuit, allowing a preparation for the driving back of the German hordes. At Mons the 1st Battalion Gordon Highlanders lost most of their officers, non-commissioned officers and men in killed, wounded and missing. This story is told by Private J. Parkinson, of the Gordons, who was invalided home at the finish of the Great Retreat.]

To be rushed from the routine of a soldier's life at home in time of peace into the thick of a fearful fight on the Continent is a strange and wonderful experience; yet it happened to me, and it was only one of many amazing experiences I went through between leaving Southampton in a transport and coming to a London hospital.

We landed at Boulogne, and went a long journey by train. At the end of it we found ourselves, on Saturday, August 22nd, billeted in a gentleman's big house and we looked forward to a comfortable night, little dreaming that so soon after leaving England we should be in the thick of a tremendous fight.

It was strange to be in a foreign country, but there was no time to dwell on that, and the British soldier soon makes himself at home, wherever he is. Those of us who were not on duty went to sleep; but we had not been resting very long when we were called to arms. That was about half-past three o'clock on the Sunday morning, August 23rd.

There was no bugle sound, no fuss, no noise; we were just quietly roused up by the pickets, and as quietly we marched out of the château and went along a big, sunken road—the main road to Paris, I think. We started at once to make trenches alongside the road, using the entrenching-tool which every soldier carries; and we went on steadily with that work for several hours on that August Sunday morning—a perfect Sabbath, with a wonderful air of peace about it. The country looked beautiful and prosperous—how soon it was to be turned into a blazing, ruined landscape, with thousands of dead and wounded men lying on it!

It would be about nine o'clock when we heard heavy firing in a wood near us—there is plenty of wooded country about Mons—and we were told that the engineers were blowing up obstacles; so we went on entrenching, for although we knew that the Germans were not far away, we had no idea they were as close as they soon proved to be.

"We were helped by the Germans throwing searchlights on us"

I am a first-class scout, and, with a corporal and three men, I was sent on picket some time before noon.

Just on the right of us was a farm, and the people who came out gave us some beer and eggs. We drank the beer and sucked the eggs, and uncommonly good they were, too, on that blazing hot August Sunday, when everything looked so pleasant and peaceful. You had it hot at home, I know; but I dare say we had it hotter, and we were in khaki, with a heavy kit to carry.

There was a big tree near us, and I made for it and climbed up, so that I could see better over the countryside. I was hanging on to a branch, and looking around, when all at once a bullet or two came, and we knew that the Germans had spotted us. I got down from that tree a vast deal quicker than I had got up into it, and we made ready to rush back to the trenches; but before scuttling we told the civilians to clear out at once, and they began to do so. The poor souls were taken aback, naturally, but they lost no time in obeying the warning, leaving all their worldly treasures—belongings which they were never to see again, for the German barbarians were soon to destroy them shamefully and mercilessly, and, worse than that, were to take the lives of innocent and inoffensive people who had not done them the slightest wrong in any way.

As soon as we had raised the alarm a whole section of Germans opened fire on the four of us, and as we could not do anything against them, being heavily outnumbered, we ran for it back to the trenches. Yes, we did run indeed, there is no mistake about that. Luckily for us we knew the way back; but if the Germans had been able to shoot for nuts with their rifles, not one of us would have been spared. We laughed as we ran, and one of the scouts, named Anderson, laughed so much that he could scarcely run, though there was nothing special to laugh at; but, as you know, there are some odd chaps amongst Highlanders. They don't care a rap for anything.

It was soon reported that there were in front of us about 15,000 Germans, including some of the finest of the Kaiser's troops, amongst them the Imperial Guard, who have worked military miracles—at peace manœuvres. And to oppose that great body of men we had only the 8th Brigade, consisting of the Royal Scots, the Royal Irish, the Middlesex—the old "Die-Hards"—and the Gordon Highlanders, of which I was in B Company.

The Royal Scots were on our right, and the Royal Irish and the Middlesex on our left. We had Royal Field Artillery, too, and never did British gunners do more splendid work and cover themselves with greater glory than in the battle of Mons.

The Royal Irish were getting their dinners when the Germans opened fire on them with their machine-guns, doing some dreadful damage straight off, for they seemed to have the range, and there was no time for the Royal Irish to get under cover.

That, I think, was really the beginning of the battle; but I had better try and give you an idea of the battlefield, so that you can understand what actually took place.

Mons itself is a fair-sized manufacturing town, with plenty of coal-mines about, and we were in a pleasant village near it, the main road to Paris cutting through the village. From our trenches we could see across the country, towards the mines and other villages, and we had a clear rifle-range of well over a mile, because a lot of obstruction in the shape of hedges, foliage and corn had been cut away.

To our rear, on each side of us, was a forest, and between the two forests were our splendid gunners, who were to do such awful mischief in the German hosts. The "Die-Hards" were in a sort of garden, and I saw only too clearly what happened to them when the fight was in full swing.

It was just before noon when the most fearful part of the battle started, and that was the artillery duel. Our own guns were making a terrible commotion near us; but the din was a very comforting sound, because it meant something very bad for the German gunners, who were making havoc in our brigade.

I saw the awful effects of the German shrapnel amongst the men of the Middlesex in that fair Belgian garden on what should have been a peaceful Sunday afternoon. The Middlesex were practically blown to pieces, and the fearful way in which they suffered was shown later, when the casualty lists were published, and it was seen that most of them were either killed, wounded or missing.

Then the Gordons' turn came. The Germans had got our position, and they opened fire on us; but we were lucky—perhaps the German batteries were too far away to be really effective. At any rate, they did not harm us much.

The battle had opened swiftly, and it continued with amazing speed and fury, for both sides soon settled into their stride—and you know, of course, that the Germans were on the promenade to Paris and were going to mop the British Army up. It took a lot of mopping!

Our own field-gunners were doing magnificently, and the Germans were first-rate hands at the deadly game. If they had been anything like as accurate with the rifle as they were with the artillery I think that very few British soldiers would have been left to tell the tale of Mons. But with the rifle they were no good.

The Germans came out of their trenches in big heaps in close formation, because their game was to rush us by sheer weight of numbers; but we just shot them down. Yet as soon as we shot them down others came out, literally like bees. No wonder the poor chaps are called by their officers "cannon-fodder"! British officers don't talk of their men in that brutal way; and the British officer always leads—shows the way; but the German officer seems to follow his men, and to shove and shoot them along.

It was marvellous to watch the Germans come on in their legions, and melt away under our artillery and rifle fire. We simply took deliberate aim at the masses of figures, grey clad, with their helmets covered with grey cloth; but it seemed as if not even our absolutely destructive fire would stop them. On they came, still on, the living actually sheltering behind the dead. But it was no use. We kept them off, and they kept themselves off, too, for it was perfectly clear that they had a horror of the bayonet, and would not come near it.

The nearest the Germans got to us, as far as I can tell—that is, to the Gordons—was about 300 yards; but that was near enough, seeing that they outnumbered us by four to one, and were amongst the finest troops of Germany. Some of the enemy's cavalry—I suppose the much-talked-of Uhlans—came into the sunken road in front of us, hoping to do business; but our machine-guns got on them, and we had a go at them with our rifles, with the result that the Uhlans made a cut for it and most of them got away. Even so, there were plenty of riderless horses galloping madly about.

Our officers had told us to carry on—and carry on we did, then and later.

What was I feeling like? Well, of course, at the start I was in a bit of a funk and it wasn't pleasant; but I can honestly say that the feeling soon vanished, as I'm certain it did from all of us, and we settled down to good hard pounding, all the time seeing who could pound the hardest and last longest. And I can assure you that, in spite of everything, men kept laughing, and they kept their spirits up.

You see, we had such splendid officers, and there is always such a fine feeling between officers and men in Highland regiments. Our colonel, a Gordon by name and commanding the Gordons, was a real gallant Gordon, who won his Victoria Cross in the South African War—a regular warrior and a veteran; amongst other things he was in at the storming of Dargai, and he had more experience of actual fighting, I should think, than all the Germans in front of us put together.

Another brave officer was Major Simpson, my company officer, a Companion of the Distinguished Service Order, which is the next best thing to the V.C. Major Simpson and a private went to fetch some ammunition. To do that they had to leave shelter and rush along in a literal hail of fire—shrapnel and bullets. It seemed as if no living thing could exist, and they were watched with intense anxiety. Shells were bursting all around us—some in the air and others on the ground, though there were German shells that did not burst at all.

Suddenly, with a fearful shattering sound, a shell burst just beside the major and the private, and for the moment it looked as if they had been destroyed. Some Gordons rushed towards them, and picked them up and put them on a horse. It was seen that they were badly hurt, but even so, and at a time like that, the major actually laughed, and I am sure he did it to keep our spirits up. He was taken away to hospital, and was laughing still when he said—

"It's all right, lads! There's nothing much the matter with me! Carry on!"

Oh, yes! There were some fine cool things done on that great Sunday when the Germans were like bees in front of us in the turnip-fields at Mons, and we were settling down into our stride.

And the N.C.O.'s were splendid, too.

Our section sergeant, Spence, when the firing was fiercest, popped up to take a shot, which is always a risky thing to do, because a bullet is so much swifter than a man's movements. The sergeant fired, and the instant he had done so he fell back into the trench, saying, "I believe they've got me now!" But they hadn't. He was taken to hospital, and it was found that a bullet had come and so cleanly grazed his head—on the left side, like this—that the hair was cut away in a little path, just like a big parting, as if it had been shaved. It was touch and go with death, the closest thing you could possibly see; but, luckily, the sergeant was all right, and he made no commotion about his narrow shave.

There was a gallant young officer and brave gentleman of the Gordons—Lieutenant Richmond—who had been doing his duty nobly throughout that Sunday afternoon.

Dusk was falling, and Lieutenant Richmond made his way out of the trench and over the open ground, crawling, to try and learn something about the Germans. He was crawling back—that is the only way in such a merciless fire—and was only about three yards from the trench when he rose up and was going to make a final dash for it. Just as he rose, a bullet struck him in the back and came out through his heart—and killed him straight away. He was in my trench, and I saw this happen quite clearly. It was such sights as that which made the Gordons all the more resolved to carry on and mow the Germans down as hard as they could—the Germans who seemed to be for ever rushing at us from the turnip-fields in front and never getting any nearer than their own barriers of dead.

I never thought it possible that such a hell of fire could be known as that which we endured and made at Mons. There was the ceaseless crackle of the rifles on both sides, with the everlasting explosions of the guns and the frightful bursting of the shells. They were particularly horrible when they burst on the cobbled road close by—as hundreds did—so near to us that it seemed as if we were certain to be shattered to pieces by the fragments of shrapnel which did so much mischief and killed so many men and horses, to say nothing of the gaping wounds they inflicted on the troops and the poor dumb beasts.

But you can best understand what the German artillery fire was like when I tell you that all the telegraph-poles were shattered, the very wires were torn away, and trees were smashed and blown to pieces. It seemed miraculous that any human being could live in such a storm of metal fragments and bullets.

From before noon until dusk, and that was a good eight hours, the battle of Mons had been truly awful; but we had held our own, and as the evening came I realised what a fearful thing a modern battle is—especially such a fight as this, brought on in a peaceful and beautiful country whose people had done no wrong.

All the villages in front of us were burning, either set on fire deliberately by the Germans, or by shells; but there was no halting in the fight, and when we could no longer see the enemy because it was dark we blazed away at the flashes of their rifles—thousands of spurts of flame; and the field-gunners crashed at the straight lines of fire which could be seen when the German artillerymen discharged their guns. We were helped, too, in a way that many of us never expected to be, and that was by the Germans throwing searchlights on us. These long, ghastly beams shone on us and gave a weird and terrible appearance to the fighters in the trenches, and more so to the outstretched forms of soldiers who had fought for the last time.

It was a dreadful yet fascinating sight, and one which I shall never forget; nor shall I ever forget the extraordinary fact that, in spite of the annihilating hail of missiles and the deafening din of battle, some of our fellows in the trenches went to sleep, and seemed to sleep as peacefully and soundly as if they were in feather beds. They went to sleep quite cheerfully, too. I should say that half our chaps were having a doze in this way and taking no notice of the fight and the screech and roar of shells and guns.

Sunday night—and such a night! The sky red with burning villages, the air rent with awful noises of guns and rifles, men and horses—a terrible commotion from the devilish fight that was going on. The villagers had left; they had fled on getting our warning, but they were not too far away to see the utter ruin of their homes.

I do not want to say too much about the villagers—it is too sad and makes one too savage; but I will tell of one incident I saw. An old man was running away, to try and get out of danger, when he was hit in the stomach. I saw him fall, and I know that he bled to death. Think of that—an absolutely innocent and inoffensive old man who had done nothing whatever to harm the brigands who were over-running Belgium!

Just about midnight we got the order to retire. We joined the survivors of the 8th Brigade and began a march which lasted nearly all night. We were weary and worn, but as right in spirit as ever, and didn't want to retire. There was no help for it, however, and the Great Retreat began. Everything that the Red Cross men could do had been done for the wounded; but there were some who had to be left, as well as the dead.

It was fearfully hot, and we were thankful indeed when we were able to lie down in a field and get about two hours' sleep—the sleep that you might suppose a log has.

When we awoke it was not to music of birds, but of shrapnel; for the Germans were following us and began to fire on us as soon as we started to retire again. Hour after hour we went on, feeling pretty bad at having to retreat; but a bit cheered when, at about two o'clock on the Monday afternoon, we began to dig trenches again. We had the field-gunners behind us once more, and joyous music it was to hear their shells screaming over our heads.

It was about dinner-time on the Monday when we had one of the most thrilling experiences of the whole fight—one of the extraordinary incidents that have become part and parcel of a modern battle, although only a very few years ago they were looked upon as mad fancies or wild dreams. We were marching along a road when we sighted a German aeroplane—a bird-like-looking thing in the sky. It was keeping watch on us, and signalling our position to the main German body. It gave the position, and the Germans promptly gave us some shells. The thing was most dangerous and unpleasant; but the German airman was not to have it all his own way.

Two of our own aeroplanes spotted him and went for him, just like immense birds—the whole business might have been carried out by living creatures of the air—and there was as fine a fight in the air as you could hope to see on land—firing and swift manœuvring with the object of killing and destroying, and both sides showing amazing pluck and skill. It was an uncommonly exciting spectacle, and it became all the more thrilling when we opened fire with our rifles.

I blazed away as hard as I could, but an aeroplane on the wing is not an easy thing to hit. Whether I struck the machine or not I can't say, but it came down in the road just where my company was. As far as I know the aeroplane was not struck—the chap that was in it planed down. He was determined not to be caught cheaply, for as soon as he landed he fired his petrol tank to destroy his machine, and then ran for it. He went off at a hard lick, but some of our cavalry rushed after him and caught him, and it was found that he was not hurt.

Just on our right was a railway, with a big cutting, and we were ordered to retire down into it; so into the cutting we got and along the line we went, retreating all that day by the railway and the roads, our gunners giving the Germans socks throughout that hard rearguard action.

On the Tuesday we were still retreating, and a miserable day it was, with a deluge of rain that soaked us to the skin. We reached a village and slept in barns, and a good sleep we got, without the trouble of undressing or drying our clothes or taking our boots off.

Early on the Wednesday morning the pickets quietly roused and warned us again, and we went out in front of the village and entrenched.

There was a big lot of coal-mines in front of us, about a mile away, with the refuse-heaps that are common to mines. Behind one of these great mounds a battery of German artillery had got into position, and one of the finest things you could have seen was the way in which our own grand gunners got on the Germans. They seemed to have found the range of the enemy exactly, and that was a good job for us, because the German shells were dropping just between us and our own artillery, and we expected to have them bang on us. But our guns silenced our opponents, and, what was more, scattered a lot of German infantry, about 1,500 yards away, who were making for us.

We got straight into our trenches, and in this respect we were lucky, because we went into one that the Engineers had made, while most of the other companies had to dig their own.

Our trench was in a cornfield. The corn had been cut down, and we spread it and other stuff in front of the trenches, on top of the earth, to make us invisible. From that queer hiding-place we resumed our blazing away at the pursuing Germans.

When Wednesday came we were at Cambrai, where hell itself seemed to be let loose again; for first thing in the morning we heard heavy artillery fire on all sides of us, and it was clear that a fearful battle was going on. We were utterly worn and weary, but were cheered by looking forward to a good dinner. We knew that the food was in the field cookers, in preparation for serving out to the men. But the dinner never came, and it was not until next day that we heard the reason why—then we learned that a German shell had blown the field cookers to smithereens.

Now all this time, from the moment the battle opened at Mons till we were blazing away again at the Germans at Cambrai we were waiting for the French to come—waiting and longing, for we were utterly outnumbered and completely exhausted; but we never had a glimpse of a Frenchman, and we know now, of course, that the French themselves were so hard pressed that they could not spare any help at all for the British.

At about half-past four in the afternoon we resumed the retreat, for a major of artillery had galloped up and shouted "Retire!" B Company retired across the level ground behind us. This was a good bit off a sunken road that we wanted to get back to, because it would give us comparative safety. Eventually we reached it, and were thankful to find that we were pretty secure, though shells were still bursting all around and over us.

From that time we never saw any more of the rest of the regiment, and I lost sight of our gallant colonel. He became numbered with the missing. There were only about 175 of my own company and parts of other companies who had got away and joined us.

A terrible time it was at Cambrai, and one that shan't forget in a hurry. The last I clearly remember of the place is that several men were killed near me; but by that time killing had become a matter of course. The Red Cross men did noble work, but they could not cover all the cases. I am sorry to say it, but it is true that the Germans deliberately fired on the hospitals at Mons and also at Cambrai. It sounds incredible, but there were many things done in Belgium by the Germans that you could not have believed unless you had seen them.

Well, from that dreadful carnage at Cambrai we went on retreating, and we never really rested until the Sunday, seven days after the battle started, when we reached Senlis, about forty miles from Paris. We had then marched between 130 and 140 miles, and had made one of the longest, hardest, swiftest and most successful retreats in history—I say successful, because Sir John French and his generals had got us out of what looked like a death-trap. We were cursing all the time we were retreating—cursing because we had to retire, though we knew that there was no help for it.

A wonderful change came with the Wednesday, because we did no more fighting. We forged ahead, blowing up bridges and doing all we could to stop the Germans.

We had a splendid time going through France, as we had had in going through Belgium, and when we reached Paris there was nothing the French people thought too good for us. We were taken across Paris in char-a-bancs, and flowers, cigarettes and five-franc pieces were thrown at us. A lot of Americans spoke to us, and were very kind. They were particularly anxious to know how we were getting on, and what we had gone through. It was very pleasant to hear our own language, as most of us did not understand a word of French.

We trained to Rouen, but had not the slightest idea that we were going to England—we thought we were being sent to hospital at Havre; but at that port we were put into motors and driven down to the quay and shoved on board a transport and brought at last to London.

I am not wounded. I was struck on the leg by a bullet, but it did not really hurt me. I was utterly worn out and exhausted, however, and rheumatism set in and crippled me, so I was sent to hospital; and here I am. But I'm almost fit and well now, and all I want to do is to fall in again before the fighting's done.

"Some of our cavalry caught him."

Chapter II – German Atrocities

George William Blow – Royal Field Artillery

*[The feeling among Allied soldiers was that the war was begun by Germany in a spirit of aggressive ruthlessness which was to spare neither man, woman nor child, and was to leave innocent people "only their eyes to weep with." The neutrality of Belgium was outraged and German hosts poured into that country. In repelling them an immortal part was played by the British Expeditionary Force, which fought against enormous odds. This story of the earlier days of the war is told from the narrative of Driver **George William Blow**, Royal Field Artillery, who was invalided home after having two of his ribs broken and five horses killed under him.]*

It was a blazing hot Sunday, and the place was Mons. We had got into camp about one on the Saturday afternoon, and had billeted till four on the Sunday morning, when we were ordered to harness up and prepare for action, but we did not receive actual fighting orders until noon; then we had to march into a place in the neighbourhood, and as soon as we reached it German shells burst over us.

That was the beginning of a long and terrible battle. We went straight into it, without any warning; but the Germans were ready, and knew what to expect, because they had been waiting for us for forty-eight hours.

It was field artillery we were up against. The Germans at that time had not got the big siege guns, which we called Black Marias, Jack Johnsons and Coal Boxes. I will tell you about them later.

We, the drivers, took the guns up into action, then we retired under cover with the horses. While we were retiring the bullets from the German shells were dropping all around us, and farther away our men at the guns and the other troops were carrying on that desperate fight against immense odds which will be always known as the battle of Mons. From start to finish we were heavily outnumbered, but we knocked them out.

We were soon hard at it, pounding away, while our infantry were simply mowing the Germans down. We had some terrible fire to put up with, and at the end of about four hours we were forced to retire from the position. At that time we were the only battery left in action out of the whole of our brigade.

An officer was sent to reconnoitre, to see where we could retire to, and he picked out a little valley, a sort of rain-wash, and the battery thundered into it. This was a hard place to tackle, and all our attention was needed to keep the horses from falling down, because the ground was so rough and steep.

So far we had not seen any of the German infantry at close quarters, but as soon as we had got into the level of the valley we ran into a lot of them, and saw that we were ambushed. In this ambush I had one of the experiences that were so common in the retreat, but I was lucky enough to come out of it safely. Many gallant deeds were done there which will never be officially known—for instance, when we were going through the valley and were being heavily fired on, and it seemed as if there was no chance for us, Corporal Holiday ran the gauntlet twice to warn us that the enemy had us in ambush.

We made a desperate effort to get out of the valley, but before we could get clear many horses were shot down, amongst them being the one I was riding. I did the only thing I could do—I lay there amongst the dead horses. I had had a narrow shave, for my cap had been shot off by a piece of shell.

The first gun and two waggons had got through, and our corporal could have got safely out, but he wasn't built that way, and wasn't thinking about himself.

He shouted, "Well, boys, your horses are down, and the best thing you can do is to run for it."

I scrambled up and dashed through some brambles—they nearly scratched me to pieces. Just as I and one or two more men got out five Germans potted at us. I had no weapon—nothing except my whip—if we had had arms we could have settled a lot of Germans that day—so I had to make a dash for cover. But the corporal, with his rifle, did splendidly, for he picked off three of the Germans, and the other two bolted.

If it had not been for the corporal I should not have been here to tell the tale; I should either have been killed or made a prisoner. Had it not been for him, in fact, they would have wiped the lot of us completely out.

We were in that deadly ambush for about five hours—from five till ten—no gunners with us, only drivers. It was night and dark, but the darkness was made terrible by the glare of the villages which the Germans had set fire to.

There we were, ambushed and imprisoned in the valley, unable to move either backward or forward, because the roadway was choked up with dead horses.

At last our major went away some distance, and inquired of a woman in a house which would be the best way for us to get out of the valley. While he was talking with her the house was surrounded by Germans, and it seemed certain that he would be discovered; but in the darkness they could not make him clearly out, and he was clever enough to shout to them in their own language. It was a critical and dangerous time, but the major scored. He baffled the Germans, and got himself out of the house, and us out of the ambush in the valley. It was a splendid performance and I believe the major was recommended for the D.S.O. on account of it.

We were thankful when we were clear of the valley, but about two miles farther on we ran into some more Germans; there were Germans everywhere, they swarmed over the whole countryside, day and night, and, as I have told you, they heavily outnumbered us all the time and at every turn. But by this time we were better able to meet them, for we had plenty of infantry with us—Gordons, and Wiltshire and Sussex men—who were joining in the retreat.

That retirement was a terrible business. Our infantry had been fighting in the trenches and in the open, and they were fighting all the time they were retiring. The Germans gave them no rest, and, like the barbarians some of them are, they showed no mercy to our wounded, as we discovered when we got back to Mons again, as we did in time. We saw lots of our wounded who had been killed by the butts of the Prussian bullies' rifles. They had the finest troops of Prussia at Mons, and I suppose the braggarts wanted to get some of their own back for having been so badly mauled by Sir John French's "contemptible little army."

In the earlier hours of the battle, during that awful Sunday at Mons and in the neighbourhood, the British had suffered heavily. Twelve men of my own battery and a dozen of the horses had been killed, and a waggon limber had been blown to pieces. Mind you, I am talking only of our own battery and our own brigade, and dealing with only a very small part of the battle. No man who shared in it can do more. Our brigade consisted of three batteries of six guns each.

It had been a day of ceaseless fighting and terrific strain on men and horses, and we were utterly done up when we got into camp at about one on the Monday morning. We hoped we might rest a bit, but we had to harness up at two, and shift off at three, because the Germans were preparing to shell the village we were in.

There was a hospital in the village, and by that time a good many of our wounded were in it. The Germans could see plainly enough that it was a hospital, and knew that it must be filled with wounded, but they deliberately shelled it and set fire to it. Our captain and my sergeant were in the hospital when the Germans fired it, but I don't know whether they got away or were left in the burning building.

By the time we were on the move again it was full daylight. We dropped into action again three or four times, but were forced to resume our retirement, harassed all the time by the Germans.

During the retirement we had several shots at German aeroplanes, which were flying about spying out our positions and signalling them to their own people; but field-guns are not much use against aircraft, because the muzzles cannot be elevated sufficiently high. You need howitzers for the work, because they are specially made for high-angle fire and can throw their shots right over aeroplanes.

We were retiring from the Monday till the Wednesday; then we got the order to drop into action again. That was at eight o'clock in the morning, and by that time we were at Cambrai, a good distance from Mons, as you can see from the map.

Mons was bad, but Cambrai was far worse. We had been retreating all the time, day and night, fighting a heavy rearguard action, so that men and horses were utterly worn out. Again the artillery did splendid work, and had to pay for it. The 6th Battery had lost two guns and a waggon at Mons, because the horses were killed, and they also had another gun put out of action. They lost a further gun at Cambrai, and the battery was almost completely cut up, but for their loss we in the 23rd Battery were able to make up in a way.

Our own guns were concealed so cleverly that the Germans could not find them anyhow. The nearest they could get to us was about fifty yards in front or fifty yards behind, and in dropping shells fifty yards make a lot of difference, as the Germans found to their cost. Our concealed battery did heavy execution amongst them, and they deserved all they got.

When I was clear of the valley I got two fresh horses; but at Cambrai, on the Wednesday, they were both killed. A shell burst and took off the head of the riding horse, and bullets killed the off horse, so I was dismounted again; and not a few of my chums were in the same unfortunate position.

Cambrai was the last battle we had before we turned the tables on the Germans, and began to drive them back at the Marne, where a tremendous fight went on for many days. Altogether we had been retiring pretty well a week, and we rejoiced when the advance began.

The advance made new men of us, especially when we saw what the Germans had done. There were plenty of wrecks of our convoys on the roads, where the enemy had got at them. That sort of thing was all right, of course, and came in fairly enough in warfare; but it made our blood boil to see the wanton damage that these so-called civilised soldiers had committed on a people who had done no greater crime than defend their hearths and families.

You ask about German cruelties and barbarities. Well, I will tell you something about what I saw myself, and people can form their own opinion as to what generally happened.

When the British troops retired from Mons the villages and the country were untouched. No words can tell how kind the Belgians and the French were to us, and I am glad to say that they were no worse for our passage through their towns and villages and farms. They gave us food and wine, and helped our sick and wounded, and wherever they were they did all they could for us.

Villages and towns and farms were peaceful and prosperous when we passed through them first; but they were terribly changed when we returned and went through them a second time, after the Germans had been at their foul work. Sword, rifle, artillery and fire had done their dreadful mischief, and deeds had been committed which filled us with horror. I will mention two or three things by way of illustration, and these are only instances of hosts of cases.

On the first day of the advance we were passing through a small village. I saw a little child which seemed to be propped up against a window. There were some infantry passing at the same time as ourselves—Gordons, I think they were—and one of the officers went into the cottage and took the little creature from the window. He found that it was dead. The Germans had killed it.

The officer had a look over the house, and in the next room he found the mother. She was dead also, and mutilated in a most ferocious way.

The interior of the cottage was in a state of absolute wreckage. The barbarians had not spared anything. They had destroyed the furniture, thrown everything about, and done their best to ruin inoffensive people whose country they had laid waste, and who had not done them the slightest wrong. When our men saw that, they went almost mad.

I will give you another instance. We passed through a village about two hours after some of the braggart Uhlans had visited it, and we saw how courageous they can be when they have only old men and women and children to deal with. They sing a different song when the British cavalry are after them. There was a farmhouse which had been the home of two old people, a farmer and his wife. I believe the poor old couple looked after the farm themselves.

We found the old lady at the farm all alone, and I saw her. A pitiful spectacle she was, and well she might be, for the Uhlans had come and taken her poor old husband out into a field and shot him, and left his dead body there. They had robbed the house of everything—all the money and every bit of food—and had left the old lady almost demented.

When our own troops came up they gave the poor old soul—she was sitting outside the house, crying—the bully beef and biscuits which had been served out to them that very morning, and which they themselves needed badly.

We heard of several cases like that from the people of the country as we returned through it, and cases of these German bullies holding revolvers to women's heads and forcing the frightened creatures to give them their rings and jewellery and everything they could lay their hands on. This was the sort of thing we saw, or heard at first hand, and it made us all the more thankful that we were driving the Germans back and getting level with them.

We fell into action that morning about seven o'clock. We had to make our way straight across country, regardless of fields or roads; and all the time the Germans shelled us. It didn't matter where we were, the shells fell beyond us; but the enemy weren't clever enough to find our twelve batteries, which were in action, and which properly "gave them socks."

We held that village till about eight o'clock, then we started on the advance again, driving the Germans back; and when once they start going they travel very quickly—when the enemy is after them.

That was the last battle we had before we got to the river Marne. So far, we had had a lot to do with the German field-guns; now we were to make the acquaintance of the bigger chaps I have referred to—Black Marias, Coal Boxes and Jack Johnsons, as I have said we called them, because they fired a big shell, a 90-pounder, which burst and made a thick cloud of filthy, greasy smoke which was enough to poison you if it got at you. I believe that the fumes of some of the German shells will actually kill you if you get them properly into your system.

The Battle of the Marne was a long and big affair, lasting about three weeks, and the Black Marias did a good deal of mischief. On the Sunday, as our ambulance waggons retired, the Germans shelled them with these siege guns, and blew them to pieces. At the finish there was not an ambulance waggon available. Yes, that is what they did, and it was done deliberately, because any soldier can tell an ambulance waggon when he sees it.

The Germans stuck at nothing to gain their ends; no trick is too dirty for them to play. One particularly vile one was the using of ambulance waggons for the purpose of carrying machine-guns. Our troops did not dream of firing at ambulance waggons; but when we saw that this wicked use was being made of them—and we did see it, for they came quite close to us—we gave the Germans in them what for.

The Germans tried three or four times to break through our lines, but our Tommies were too good for them, and sent them back a great deal faster than they had come on. They swept them away with rifle fire, and the Germans never had a chance when our men could get fairly in with the bayonet.

During that long month of fighting we were in a good many places in France and Belgium. At one time we were actually on the field of Waterloo, and could see in the distance the monument put up in memory of the battle. I dare say the Germans fancied they were going to do a lot with us at Waterloo; but it all ended in fancy, and we kept on the driving game with them till they were altogether forced back.

When we could get at them we could beat them, though they were sometimes about ten to one, and in one little affair I saw twenty of our "Jocks"—Gordons, I think they were—scatter something like two hundred Germans. The Jocks badly wanted to get at the Germans with the steel, but the Germans just as badly didn't want to be bayoneted, and those who weren't shot scuttled.

The fighting was not the only hard part of the Battle of the Marne. For nearly three weeks we never had a dry shirt on owing to the wet weather, and we never had our boots off; we hadn't time for it, and we were kept too well at it. The poor horses were fearfully knocked up. They were like us—never had a chance to rest—and were three or four days without food.

Once, during the retirement, we had only two hours' rest in four days; but we daren't stop. Sometimes we were on foot, sometimes in the saddle, and the Germans were after us in motor-lorries, full of troops.

But however badly they handled us, I think it was nothing to the way in which we mangled them when our artillery got really to work, and especially when it came to "gun fire"—that is, rapid firing, each gun firing as soon as it is loaded. This means that you take no time between rounds; you simply blaze away, and the guns become quite hot. In one particular position every subsection fired 150 rounds, so that, taking a whole battery, I should think they pretty well fired a thousand rounds in a day.

It was on the Marne that my fifth horse was killed under me. A shell struck him, and before I could clear myself I fell over into a ditch, the horse on top of me, shot and shell flying all around as I went over. Two of my ribs were broken, and I was put out of action. I was picked up and carried down to the camp. I was in hospital there for three days before I was sent to London.

I had a complete Uhlan's uniform with me, and wanted to bring it home, but this bit of the saddle is all I have left. The Uhlan's saddle is a wonderful thing, weighing 78 lb., compared with 12 lb. for the British saddle. Here is the piece; you can see that it is filled in with lead—why, I don't know. And here is the torn khaki jacket I was wearing when my fifth horse was killed under me at the Marne—and this part is sodden with his blood.

I had a round month of fighting, retreating, advancing, and fighting again, and apart from the broken ribs I was utterly done up; but I am pretty well again now. I am just off to see the doctor; the day after to-morrow I am to get married, the next day I rejoin, and after that—well, who can tell?

A WW1 era Lee Enfield rifle with bayonet detached - Image: Vaarok

Chapter III - "Greenjackets" in the Firing Line

Rifleman R. Brice, King's Royal Rifle Corps

[The King's Royal Rifle Corps, the famous old 60th Rifles, the "Greenjackets," I have had a large share in the war and have added to their glorious distinctions. Many of the officers of this regiment have given their lives for their country, amongst them being Prince Maurice of Battenberg. Some details of the Prince's service in the war before he was killed in action are given in this story by Rifleman Brice, of the 60th, who was wounded at the Battle of the Aisne and invalided home.]

WHEN we first landed in France we were welcomed and cheered by crowds of French people who decked us with flowers and couldn't do too much for us, and they kept that kindness up all the time I was over there until I was sent home with a lot more wounded. Throwing flowers at us was a great deal pleasanter than the shells and bullets which were shot at us a few days later, when we were in the thick of trench-digging and fighting. It's astonishing how soon you settle down to a state of things that you've never been used to and how extraordinarily war alters life and people.

The Greenjackets are very proud of themselves, especially in time of peace, and have many little ways of their own; but a war like this makes all soldiers chums and equals and even the officers are practically just like the men. Our own colonel did his share in the trench-digging, and a royal officer like Prince Maurice of Battenberg, who is now resting in a soldier's grave, was living the same life as the rest of us. Many an act of kindness did the Prince show to his riflemen, and many a fierce fight he shared in before he was killed in battle; many a word of cheer did he utter to men who were almost exhausted and nearly dying of thirst, and I have seen him go and buy fresh bread, when it could be got, and give it to us as a treat—and a glorious treat it was!

One of the first things we had to do after the retirement from Mons was to bury German dead, and you will get some idea of the awful losses they suffered, even at the beginning of the war, when I tell you that in one place alone we were about eight hours in doing this unpleasant task.

We got used to digging ourselves in and being shelled out, and to guarding towns and villages while the panic-stricken inhabitants escaped to safety. It was a pitiful sight to see people turned out of their houses, taking their belongings, when they could, in carts, perambulators, wheelbarrows and every available conveyance. They always kept as close to us as they could keep, and our fellows used to collect money amongst themselves for the poor souls and give them all the food they could spare—and they were very grateful if we gave them only a biscuit.

It was terrible work on our way to the Aisne; but the hardships were lightened for us in many little ways that counted a lot. Some of our officers would carry two rifles, when men became too weary to carry their own; the colonel would jump off his horse and give an exhausted man a lift in the saddle, and he would take apples from his pockets and pass them along the ranks to the men. These acts of kindness helped us all enormously. And we were helped on the way by smoking—what a joy it was to get a fag, especially when cigarettes ran so short that one would go round a dozen times, passed from man to man, and a chap was sorely tempted to take a pull that was almost enough to fill him with smoke. When we hadn't a scrap of tobacco of any sort we would roll a fag of dried tea-leaves which had been used for making tea—and that was better than nothing.

It was fighting all the way to the Aisne, heavy rearguard actions most of the time, though in a lesser war many of these affairs would have been reckoned proper battles. One night, at about ten o'clock, after a hard march, we had reached a town, and had thankfully gone into our billets—houses, barns, any sort of place that came handy, and we were expecting a peaceful time; but we were no sooner settling than we got the alarm to dress and fall in. Getting dressed was the work of seconds only, because undressing was merely a case of putting the pack and equipment and rifle down and resting on the flags or earth, or, if we were lucky, hay or straw; and so, when the alarm was given, we very soon fell in, and with fixed bayonets we rushed for a bridge across the river that we had been ordered to take.

At the point of the bayonet the bridge was carried with a splendid rush, then we had to hold it while our transport and ammunition column got out of the town, and there we were till seven o'clock next morning. The main body of the troops retired and left us as a rearguard; but they had not gone from the town more than ten minutes when we saw the Germans coming towards the bridge in swarms. There was no help for it—we had to get away from the bridge which we had held throughout the night.

We began to retire in good order, fighting desperately, and our men falling killed and wounded. Yard by yard we fell back from the bridge, firing as furiously as we could at the German masses, and for half a mile we kept up an unequal rearguard struggle. It seemed that we should be hopelessly outnumbered and that there was little hope; then we saw two divisions of the French advancing, and knew that we should pull through. The French came on and gave us help, and, covering our retirement, enabled us to get away from the bridge.

It was in one of the charges on a bridge which was held by the Germans, just before we got to the Aisne, that Prince Maurice distinguished himself. He was very daring and was always one of the first in the fighting, no matter where or what it was. I was not actually in the charge, being in the supports behind; but I saw the charge made, and a grand sight it was to watch our fellows rush forward with the steel and take the bridge. At another time the Prince was in action with a German rearguard and narrowly escaped death. I was in this affair, and saw a German shell burst about a yard away. It plugged into the ground and made a fine commotion and scattered earth and fragments around us; but a chum and myself laughed as we dodged it, and that was the way we got into of taking these explosions when we became used to the war. You could not help laughing, even if you were a bit nervous. During this fight Prince Maurice was shot through the cap, so that he had a shave for his life, but he made light of his escape, and was very proud of the hole in the cap, which he showed to us when he talked with us, as he often did, before he fell.

There were so many incidents of coolness and disregard of wounds that it is not easy to recollect them all; but I call to mind that our adjutant, Lieutenant Woods, was shot in a little affair with the Germans. A sergeant had taken a maxim gun to put in position at a certain spot; but he had gone the wrong way and the adjutant went after him to put things right. He was too late, however, for the sergeant was spotted by the Germans and was killed. The adjutant himself was struck, but managed to get away, and he came back laughing and saying, "Oh! damn those Germans! They've shot me in the leg!" But in spite of the wound he would not lie up or let anybody do anything for him—he bound up the wound himself and carried on.

I saw another case, later, which illustrates the coolness of the British officer and his determination not to leave the fight till he is forced to do so. I was by that time wounded and in a temporary hospital, and the artillery were keeping up one of the endless duels. The officer had been struck, and he came into the hospital, and I saw that his hand had been partially blown off; but instead of caving in, as he might well have done, he had the hand bound up and put it in a sling, then he went back to his battery just outside the windows and kept on pounding away at the Germans.

We had plenty of excitement with the German aeroplanes, and often potted at them, but I did not see any of the machines brought down. I remember one day when an aeroplane was trying to locate our position—we were retiring through a French village—and a brigade started firing at it. Just when the aeroplane appeared, the little boys and girls of the village were giving us delicious plums, which they were getting from the trees. We were thoroughly enjoying ourselves, and the youngsters liked it too, when the aeroplane swooped along and we instantly started firing at it. So many rifles going made a tremendous rattle, and the poor little boys and girls were terrified and ran off screaming, and scattered in all directions. We shouted to them and tried to bring them back, but they didn't come, and disappeared in all sorts of hiding-places. The aeroplane got away, I believe, but at any rate it did no mischief at that particular spot. The French civilian folk got used to running off and hiding. In another village we passed through we came to a large house and found that three young ladies and their parents had been forced into the cellar and locked there by the Germans. When we entered the house, the prisoners were starving, and were thankful for anything that we gave them; but they would not take any money from us. The young ladies spoke English quite nicely.

We got quite used to aeroplanes—our own, the Germans, and the French, and saw several thrilling fights in the air. Once we saw a French aeroplane furiously fired on by the Germans—a regular cannonade it was; but the shells and bullets never got at it, and the aeroplane escaped. It was wonderful to see the way the machine shot down, as if nothing could prevent it from smashing on the ground, then to watch it suddenly turn upward and soar away as safely and swiftly as a bird. The airman's idea seemed to be to dodge the fire, and he darted about in such a bewildering fashion that no gunner or rifleman could hope to do anything with him. We were all greatly excited by this thrilling performance in the air, and glad when we knew that the plucky Frenchman had been swift enough to dodge the shells and bullets.

We had had some very trying work to do, and now we were going to get our reward for it. Some of the hardest of the work was that about which people hear nothing, and perhaps never even think—on sentry at night, for instance, about the most nerve-racking job you can imagine. We were always double sentry, and stood for two hours about five yards from each other, like statues, never moving. I always felt funky at this sort of work at the start—you can imagine such a lot in the dark and the strain is so heavy. At the slightest sound the rifle would be presented, and the word "Halt!" ring out—just that word and nothing more, and if there wasn't an instant satisfactory reply it was a bad look-out for the other party. The Germans were very cunning at getting up to some of the British outposts and sentries, and as so many of them speak English very well, they were dangerous customers to tackle, and this added to the heavy strain of sentry work at night.

Now I come to the Battle of the Aisne. I had three days and nights of it before I was bowled out.

A strange thing happened on the first day of the battle, and that was the appearance of a little black dog. I don't know where he came from, or why he joined us, but he followed the battalion all the rest of the time I was with it, and not only that, but he went into action, so he became quite one of us.

Once, in the darkness, we walked into a German outpost. We found it pretty hard going just about there, for the German dead were so thick that we had to walk over them. That march in the night was a wonderful and solemn thing. Three columns of us were going in different directions, yet moving so quietly that you could scarcely hear a sound. All around us, in that Valley of the Aisne, were burning buildings and haystacks, making a terrible illumination, and showing too well what war means when it is carried on by a nation like the Germans, for this burning and destroying was their doing.

Silently, without any talking, we went on, and then we fell into the outpost. I heard the stillness of the night broken by the sharp sound of voices, a sound which was instantly followed by shots, and the furious barking of our little dog, which up to that point had been perfectly quiet. The shots were fired by Captain Woollen, who killed two of the Germans, and one of our men shot a third. We left them where they fell and retired as quickly as we could; but we had done what we started out to do, and that was to find the position of the enemy.

While advancing again we caught a column of Germans. Our brigade-major saw them and came tearing back and told us that they were about fourteen hundred yards to the left of us. Within ten minutes we had a firing line made and our artillery was in position as well. It was a grand sight to see our fellows running into the firing line smoking cigarettes, as cool as if they were doing a bit of skirmishing on training.

We gave the Germans about three hours' hot firing, then a company went round to take the prisoners. The white flag had been shown, but we had not been allowed to take any notice of that until we were sure of our men, because the Germans had so often made a wrong use of the signal of surrender. When the company got round to the Germans it was found that they had already thrown down their rifles. Our brigade took about 500 prisoners, and the rest we handed over to the 1st Division. The Germans had about a mile and a half of convoy, which got away; but the French captured it in the evening, and so made a very nice little complete victory of the affair.

At that time, early in the war, the Germans thought they were going to have it all their own way, and they considered that any trick, white flag or otherwise, was good enough. So certain were they about victory that in one village we passed through we saw written on a wall, in English, evidently by a German, "We will do the tango in Paris on the 13th." We laughed a good deal when we read that boast, and well we might, for it was on the 13th that we saw the writing on the wall, and the Germans by that time were getting driven a long way back from the French capital.

On the Monday morning we went out as flank guard on the Aisne, and were going along behind some hills when our captain spotted swarms of Germans coming up over a ridge about twelve hundred yards away. He ordered two platoons to go out and line the ridge, and for the ridge we went. When we reached it, our captain told us that not a man was to show his head over the ridge until he gave the word to fire.

The Germans came on, getting nearer and nearer, in dense masses, and it was the hardest thing in the world not to let fly at them. They advanced till they were about seven hundred yards away, then we showed them what British rifles could do. We simply went for them, and our rifles got so hot that we could scarcely hold them. Despite that awful hail of bullets the Germans came on, and hurled themselves against us till they were not more than a hundred yards away; then we wanted to charge them, and begged to be let loose with the bayonet, but our captain told us that there were not enough of us to do it. So we retired to our own battalion, the whole of which had the joy of going for them. But the Germans didn't wait for us. They don't like the British steel, and when we had pushed them right back, without actually getting at them, they cleared off.

This was the kind of thing that went on in the Valley of the Aisne. It was work in the open and work in the trenches, on top of the incessant fighting we had had. On the third day, at night, we had just come out of the trenches, having been relieved by another company. We were in good spirits, for we had been sent to a barn, where we were to spend the night. That was a splendid bit of luck, because it meant that we were to get a nice rest and have a good time. The barn had hay in it, and we simply packed the place. It was on a farm, and during the day we had seen the farmer and his wife. There was a village near, with a church and houses, and it had proved a fine target for the Germans, who constantly shelled the place. We had got quite into the way of watching the shells burst about fifty yards in front of us, and it really was a grand sight to sit and gaze at them. We sometimes did this when we were so heavily bombarded that we could do nothing with the rifle or bayonet. Little did we know what was in store for us at the barn from shells.

The Germans came on and hurled themselves against us.

The night passed and the morning came. We breakfasted and made ready to march; but were ordered to hold back a bit, and so we put aside our packs and rifles and had a sing-song to pass the time. It was one of the most surprising concerts ever held, I daresay, because all the time about three German batteries were shelling us, and occasionally a shell burst very near us and made an awful commotion. We were still packed in the barn, quite cheerful, when the sergeant who was in charge of us, and was acting as sergeant-major, told us to fall in.

He had hardly spoken the words when the very building seemed to collapse, the wall was blown in, the roof fell, timbers crashed down and the barn was filled with a horrible smoke and dust, and there were deafening and awful cries—screams and groans where a few moments earlier there had been the sound of merriment, for a German shell had crashed through the wall and exploded in the very thick of us.

I was lying down in the barn, with my pack on, when this thing happened. I sprang to my feet and dashed to the door and rushed into the open air, but as soon as I had left the building a second shell came and burst and I was knocked down. I tried to rise, but my leg was numb, and so I had to wait till the stretcher-bearers came and took me to a big white house about three hundred yards away, which had been turned into a hospital, and there I was put with the rest of the wounded. For about ten minutes I had to wait outside, and there I was struck by a piece of spent shell, but not much hurt. When we were carried off in the stretchers we were kept near the bank of the road, to avoid as much as possible the German fire.

At the hospital it was found that I had been wounded in the leg; but I did not care so much about myself, I wanted to know what had happened in the barn. I soon learned the dreadful truth—the shells had killed eleven of the men and wounded thirty-two, some of whom died afterwards.

Prince Maurice was close at hand when this happened, and at night he attended the burial of the poor fellows near the barn. About an hour after the men were killed he came into the house to see us. "How are you getting on?" he asked me. "I am so sorry such a dreadful thing has happened." And he looked it, too.

I was in the hospital three days before being sent home. All that time there were villagers in the cellars of the hospital, terrified people who were hiding from the German fire, and were fed from our transport.

A lot was crowded into that retirement from Mons and the advance to the Aisne. We had kept our spirits up and had not been downhearted, and when the great day came which brought the order to advance and fight the enemy, we positively shouted and sang. And this was not just swank; it was a real expression of our feelings, for we wanted to do our bit for the Empire.

Chapter IV - The Struggle on the Aisne

Private Herbert Page, Coldstream Guards.

[*The Battle of the Aisne began on Sunday, September 13th, 1914, when the Allies crossed the river. The Germans made furious efforts to hack their way through to Paris, but after a struggle lasting three weeks they were driven back with enormous losses. The British losses were: 561 officers and 12,980 men in killed, wounded and missing. The beginning of this tremendous conflict is told by Private Herbert Page, of the Coldstream Guards, who was wounded and had a wonderful escape from instant death on the battlefield.*]

THERE was fierce fighting all day on Sunday, September 13th, when the Battle of the Aisne began; but the Coldstreamers were not in it till the Monday. We had had a lot of heavy fighting, though, since the beginning of the business at Mons, and we had had a fine fight at Landrecies—a fight which has been specially mentioned in despatches. At the end of it all the men in my company—Number 2—had their names taken, but I don't know why. Anyway, it was a grand affair, and no doubt someday the real full story of it will be told and everybody will know what the Coldstreamers did there. Landrecies is particularly an affair of the 3rd Coldstreamers.

We had had a very hard time, fighting and marching and sleeping in the open during the cold nights and in thick mud or in trenches that were deep in water; but with it all we kept very cheerful, especially when we knew that we had brought the Germans up with a jerk and were beginning to roll them back.

The Coldstreamers were in the open all day on the Sunday, right on the side of the artillery, behind a big hill, and were very comfortable. The artillery on both sides were hard at it, but the Germans could not get our range and no shells came near us. It was harvest time, and we were lying down on sheaves of wheat, and making ourselves as cosy as we could. That was not altogether easy to do, because it was raining during the best part of the day and everything was rather depressing and very wet. But we put our oilsheets on the ground, our greatcoats over the oilsheets, and straw on the top of ourselves, so that we were really pretty snug, taken altogether. The straw, I fancy, was put there not so much to give us comfort as to hide us from the view of the chaps who were always flying about in the German aeroplanes, trying to spot us and make our positions known to their own gunners.

Our own aeroplanes and the Germans' were very busy during that Sunday, and shells were flying about them on both sides, but I don't think they were doing much mischief. We ourselves were doing very nicely indeed. Our transport came up and issued new biscuits, and we got a pot of jam each—and delicious they were, too. We enjoyed them immensely, and didn't care a rap about the German shells. Our transport was splendid, and we always had something to go on with. There was no fixed time for any meal, there couldn't be, for we used to march about fifty minutes and take ten minutes' halt. If we were on a long day's march we would get an hour or two at dinner-time, usually from one o'clock. It was a funny country we were in, hot in the daytime and cold at night; but we soon got used to that. We were helped enormously by the kindness of the French, and we got on very well with the people and had not much difficulty in making ourselves understood, especially as we picked up a few words of the language—and we could always make signs. When we wanted a drink we would hold out our water-bottles and say "loo," and they laughed and rushed off and filled our bottles with water.

On the way to the Valley of the Aisne we passed through towns and villages where the Germans had been and we saw what outrages they had committed on both people and property. They had recklessly destroyed everything. They had thrown poor people's property out of the windows into the streets and pulled their bedding into the roads to lie on themselves. The Germans acted like barbarians wherever they went—I saw one poor child who was riddled with bullets. We ourselves had strict orders against looting of any sort, but we did not dream of touching other people's property. Whenever we came to a town or village we warned the people to get away, as the Germans were coming, and they went. It was always pleasant to hear them say—as they did to our officers, who spoke to them in French—that they felt safe when the English were there.

The river Aisne runs through lovely country, which looks a bit of a wreck now, because we had to rush across the open and trample down the wheat to get at the Germans. The country's crops were spoiled, but the damage we did was trifling compared with the devastation that the Germans caused.

Throughout that Sunday when the Battle of the Aisne opened we had no casualties, and the day passed pretty well. At night we slept in a barn, which was better than the wet fields. There were no rats, but plenty of rabbits, for the people of the farm seemed to breed them and to have left the hutches open. That night in the barn gave me the best rest I had had since Mons, as I was not even on guard. We had a good breakfast in the barn, tea, bully beef and biscuits, and marched off soon after six in the morning, which was very wet and cold. We marched about four miles, until we came to the Aisne, to a bridge that had been blown up and so shattered that there was only a broken girder left. The rest of the bridge was in the river, which was very deep in the middle, after the heavy rains.

We were now properly in the thick of the battle and a fierce business it was, because the Germans had the range of us and were dropping shells as fast as they could fire. Some of the Guards were got across by boats, but we had to wait our turn to cross over a pontoon bridge which the Engineers had put up, in spite of the heavy fire.

We felt the German artillery fire at this place, near the village of Vendresse, but we could not see them. We watched the Loyal North Lancashires cross the pontoon bridge and saw them march away on the other side of the river, which was well wooded, then we heard them firing hard and knew that they were in action with the Germans. We were not long in following the North Lancashires and over the pontoon bridge we went, going very quietly, as we had been told to make as little noise as possible. In about an hour we were properly in the business ourselves.

After crossing the river we began to feel that at last we were really at the Germans. We made the best of the shelter that the wood gave us, and from behind trees and from the sodden ground we kept up a destructive fire on the enemy, getting nearer to him all the time. Things were growing very hot and the whole countryside rang with the crashing of the guns and the everlasting rattle of the rifles and machine-guns. We were expecting more of our men to cross the river and reinforce us, but the German guns had got the range of the pontoons and no more of our men could cross, so that for the time being we were cut off and had to do as best we could with one of the very strong rear-guards of the enemy.

When we had put some good firing in from the wood we left the shelter of the trees and got into the open country, and then we were met by a shell fire which did a great deal of mischief amongst us. These shells were the big chaps that we called Jack Johnsons, and one came and struck an officer of the North Lancashires who was standing on the right of his line. I was not far from him, being on the left of our own line. The shell shattered both his legs and he fell to the ground. I hurried up, and the first thing the officer asked for was a smoke. We propped him up against a haycock and a chap who had some French tobacco made a fag and gave it to the officer—nobody had a cigarette readymade. He smoked half of it and died. By that time the stretcher-bearers had come up and were taking him away. Before he left for the rear I gently pulled his cap over his face. This affair filled the men around with grief, but it put more heart into us to go on fighting the Germans.

Our artillery now began to fire rapidly and the Germans started to retire. There was a big bunch of them, and they made for the hill as fast as they could go, meaning to scuttle down the other side and get away. But our gunners were too sharp for them, and they were properly roused up by that time. They came up in splendid style—the 117th Field Battery, I think they were—and just as the Germans reached the top of the hill in a solid body our gunners dropped three shells straight into them, and three parts of the flying Germans stopped on the top of the hill—dead.

I could not say how many Germans there were against us at this place, but I know that they came on in swarms, and they went down as fast as we could fire. But their going down seemed to make no difference to their numbers. They were only a few hundred yards away, and we could see them quite plainly. They were running all over the place, like a lot of mad sheep, they were so excited. And they were blowing trumpets, like our cavalry trumpets, and beating drums and shouting "Hoch! Hoch!" as hard as they could shout.

They kept blowing their charge and banging their drums till they were about 300 yards away, and shouting their "Hochs!" They shouted other words as well, but I don't know what they were.

When our chaps heard the trumpets and drums going and the German cheers they answered with a good old British "Hooray!" and a lot of them laughed and shouted, "Here comes the Kaiser's rag-time band! We'll give you 'Hoch!' when you get a bit nearer!" And I think we did. At any rate we kept on firing at them all the time they were advancing; but they swept ahead in such big numbers that we were forced to retire into the wood.

As soon as we got into the wood we came under very heavy machine-gun fire from the Germans, and the bullets rained about us, driving into the earth and into the trees and whizzing all around us everywhere. The German shells were smashing after us, too, but were not doing much damage at that point.

It was now that I lost a very old chum of mine, a fine chap from Newcastle named Layden, a private. He was in the thick of the machine-gun fire, a few paces from me, when he suddenly cried out and I knew that he was hit. The first thing he said was, "Give me a cigarette. I know I shan't go on much longer." When we asked him what the matter was he said he was hurt. "Are you wounded?" he was asked. "Yes, I'm hit in the stomach," he answered—and he was, by about seventeen bullets.

The call went round for a cigarette, but nobody had one—lots of cigarettes were sent out to the soldiers that never reached them—but poor Layden was soon beyond the need of fags. He was delirious when our stretcher-bearers came and took him to a barn which had been turned into a temporary hospital. He lingered there for some time; but the last I saw of him was on the field. I missed him badly, because we had been good chums, and whatever we got we used to give each other half of it.

For about five hours, until two o'clock in the afternoon, that part of the battle went on, and all the time we were holding the Germans back; then we were reinforced by the remainder of our troops, who came across the pontoon bridge to our assistance.

The Germans now seemed to think that they had had enough of it and they held up white flags, and we left the shelter of the wood and went out to capture them. I should think that there were about three hundred of the Germans at that point who pretended to surrender by holding up the white flag; but as soon as we were up with them their people behind fired at us—a treacherous trick they practised very often. In spite of it all we managed to get the best part of the prisoners safe and drove them in before us to our own lines. When they really surrendered, and did not play the white flag game, we used to go up and take all their rifles, bayonets and ammunition, and throw them away out of their reach, so that they could not make a sudden dash for them and turn on us. When we had chased a few prisoners and had seen what the Germans meant by the white flag signal, we were told to take no notice of it, but to keep on shooting till they put their hands up.

A lot of the prisoners spoke English and said how glad they were to be captured and have no more fighting to do. Some said they loved England too much to want to fight against us, and a German said, "Long live King George, and blow the Kaiser!" But I don't know how many of them meant what they said—you can't depend on Germans.

We had plenty of talks with the German prisoners who could speak English. Some of them who had lived in England spoke our language quite well, and it was very interesting to hear what they had to say about us and the French and the Belgians. They couldn't stand the British cavalry, and one man said, "We don't like those Englishmen on the grey horses at all," meaning the Scots Greys. Several of the prisoners said they didn't mind so much fighting the French, because the French infantry fired too high, nor the Russians, because they fired too low; "but," they said, "every time the Englishman pulls the trigger he means death." That was a very nice compliment to us, and there was a great deal of truth in what was said about the British rifle fire. I can assure you that when we settled down to the work we often enough plugged into the Germans just as if we were on manœuvres.

At the very first—and I'm not ashamed to say it—I shook like a leaf and fired anyhow and pretty well anywhere; but when that first awful nervousness had passed—not to return—we went at it ding-dong all the time and fired as steadily as if we were on the ranges. The men were amazingly cool at the business—and as for the officers, well, they didn't seem to care a rap for bullets or shells or anything else, and walked about and gave orders as if there were no such things in the world as German soldiers.

Most of the poor beggars we took were ravenous for want of food, and those who could speak English said they had been practically without food for days, and we saw that they had had to make shift with the oats that the horses were fed with. This starvation arose from the fact that a few days earlier we had captured the German transport and left them pretty short of food.

That rush after the Germans and bagging them was exciting work. It was successful and everything seemed to be going very well. But there was a nasty surprise in store for me and one which very nearly ended my career as a fighting man. I had really a miraculous escape.

I had charge of about four prisoners, and kept them well in front of me, so that they could not rush me. I kept them covered with my rifle all the time, and as I had ten rounds in my magazine I knew that they wouldn't have a ghost of a chance if they tried any German tricks on me—I could easily have finished the lot before they could have got at me.

As I was driving the prisoners I felt as if someone had come up and punched me on the ear. I did not know whether I had been actually hit by somebody or shot, but I turned my head and at once fell to the ground. I was swiftly up again on my feet and scrambled about. I knew that I was hurt, but the thing I mostly cared about just then was my bag of prisoners, so I handed them over to another man, and he took them in. I then found that I had been shot in the neck by a bullet. It had gone in at the collar of the jacket, at the back of the neck—here's the hole it made—and through the neck and out here, where the scar is, just under the jaw. A narrow shave? Yes, that's what the doctor said—it had just missed the jugular vein. The shot bowled me out, but it was a poor performance by the German who fired, because he could not have been more than three hundred yards away, and being six foot one I made a big target at that short distance. Anyway, he missed me and I was told to go to a barn not far away which had been turned into a hospital, bed mattresses having been placed on the floor.

Here my kit was taken off me and I was looked after at once, my kit being given to a North Lancashire man who had lost his own and had been without one for three days. He had been in a small battle and had had to take his choice between dropping his kit and being caught; so he got rid of his kit and was able to escape. When he left the barn he went into the firing line, but he only lasted about ten minutes there. I had seen him leave and I saw him brought back by the stretcher-bearers. As soon as he was inside the barn he asked where I was, and he was told and was laid down close to me. "Look here, old chap," he said pleasantly, "if you'd only been ten minutes later I shouldn't have been here, because I shouldn't have got your kit and gone into the firing line and got hit."

From behind trees we kept up a destructive fire on the enemy

Perhaps he was right. He might have escaped; but as it was he had been shot through both legs.

I didn't like being in the barn and out of the fighting. It was better to be in the firing line, with all its excitement and the knowledge that you were doing your bit to help things along and drive the Germans back to the best place for them, and that's Germany; but our officers, who never lost a chance of cheering and helping us, came in when they could to see how we were getting on. During the afternoon my company officer, Captain Brocklehurst, and the adjutant, came in to see how things were going. Captain Brocklehurst saw me and said, "There are not many of the company left; but we're doing wonderfully well. We've killed a good many of the Germans and taken about five hundred prisoners." That was good news, very good, but it was even better when the captain added, "And we're pushing them back all the time."

The guns were booming and the rifles were crackling all around us while we were lying in the barn, and wounded men were being constantly brought in, keeping the doctors and the ambulance men terribly busy—and you can imagine what it must have meant for the Germans if it was like that for us; because we fought in open order, so that we were not easy to hit, whereas the

Germans were in their solid formation, which meant that they could not advance against the British fire without being mown down.

I was in the barn, which was crowded with wounded, till about one o'clock in the morning, then we were taken in Red Cross vans to another hospital about three miles away, and as we left the French people showed us all the kindness they could, giving us water, milk and food, in fact all they had. We crossed the pontoon bridge and were put into another barn which had been turned into a hospital, and we stayed there for the night. We left that place in the morning for La Fère, about twenty miles away. There were a great many motor waggons being used as ambulances, and they were all needed, because of the crowds of wounded. All of us who could walk had to do so, as all the vans and lorries were wanted for the bad cases. I could manage to walk for about a mile at a stretch, but I could not use my arms. When I had done a mile, I rested, then went on again, and so I got to the end of the journey, with a lot more who were just about able to do the same. We didn't grumble, because we were thankful to be able to walk at all and not to be so badly wounded that we could not shift for ourselves. When we got to La Fère the hospital was so full that we were put straight into a hospital train, and I was in it for two days and nights, stopping at stations for brief halts. Again the French people were kindness itself and pressed food and drink on us. We got to Nantes, where my wound was dressed and we had supper, and then I had what seemed like a taste of heaven, for I was put into a proper bed. Yes, after sleeping for so many nights on the ground, anyhow and anywhere, often enough in mud and water, it was like getting into heaven itself to get into a bed. On the Saturday they put us on board a ship and took us round to Liverpool, a four days' journey on the sea. First we went to Fazackerley, and then I was lucky enough to be sent on to Knowsley Hall, where Lady Derby, who has a son in France with the Grenadiers, had turned the state dining-room into a hospital ward. There were sixteen Guardsmen in the ward, with four trained nurses to look after us. Wasn't that a contrast to the barns and flooded trenches! Now I'm back in London, feeling almost fit again, and soon I shall have to report myself.

I have only told you about the little bit I saw myself of the tremendous Battle of the Aisne. Considering the length of it and the fearful nature of the firing, it sometimes strikes me as a very strange thing that I should be alive at all; but stranger still that some men went through it all, right away from the beginning at Mons, and escaped without a scratch.

Chapter V – "The Most Critical Day of All"

Corporal F. W. Holmes, V.C., M.M., 2nd Battalion King's Own Yorkshire Light Infantry.

[In the first four months of the war nineteen Victoria Crosses were gazetted for valour in the field, and of these no fewer than five were awarded for the sanguinary fighting at Le Cateau on August 26th, 1914. In his despatch dealing with the retreat from Mons Sir John French described the 26th as "the most critical day of all." It was during this crisis of the battle that Corporal Frederick William Holmes, of the 2nd Battalion The King's Own (Yorkshire Light Infantry), "carried a wounded man out of the trenches under heavy fire and later assisted to drive a gun out of action by taking the place of a driver who had been wounded." Corporal Holmes has not only won the Victoria Cross, but he has been also awarded the Médaille Militaire of the Legion of Honour of France. His story gives further proof of the wondrous courage and endurance of the gallant British Army in Belgium and in France.]

F OR seven years I was with the colours in the old 51st, which is now the Yorkshire Light Infantry, then I was drafted to the Reserve; but I was called back only a fortnight later, when the war broke out.

The regimental depôt is at Pontefract, in South Yorkshire, which some unkind people say is the last place that God started and never finished, and in August, having become a soldier again, after marrying and settling down to civil life in Dublin, I found myself in a region which was almost like the South Yorkshire coalfields. There were the same pit-heads and shale-heaps, so that you could almost think you were in England again—but how different from England's calmness and security! It was around these pit-heads and shale-heaps that some of the fiercest fighting of the earlier days of the war took place.

We had left Dublin and reached Havre at midnight; we had been to the fortified town of Landrecies, where the Coldstreamers were to do such glorious things, and had got to Maroilles, where Sir Douglas Haig and the 1st Division became heavily engaged. We were at Maroilles, in billets, from the 18th to the 21st. Billets meant almost anything, and we lived and slept in all sorts of places as well as the trenches—but being in the open in summer was no hardship. The fields had been harvested and we often slept on the stacks of corn.

The people were really most kind; they gave us every mortal thing as we marched, beer, wine, cigarettes and anything else there was.

At five o'clock on the Saturday afternoon we were billeted in a brewery, where we stayed till Sunday noon, when, as we were having dinner, shells were bursting and beginning things for us. We were ordered to take up a position about two miles from Mons, and on that famous Sunday we went into action near a railway embankment.

People by this time know all about Mons, so I will only say that after that hard business we retired towards Le Cateau, after fighting all day on the 24th and all the following night. After that we took up a position on outpost and stayed on outpost all night, then, at about two in the morning, we dropped into some trenches that we had previously occupied.

I know what Mons was and I went through the battles of the Marne and the Aisne; but nothing I had seen could be compared for fury and horror with the stand of the 5th Division on the 26th. It was essentially a fight by the 5th, because that was the only division employed at Le Cateau. The division was composed of three brigades, the 12th, 13th and 14th. My battalion, the 2nd Yorkshire Light Infantry, was in the 13th, the other battalions with us being the West Riding, the King's Own Scottish Borderers and the West Kent.

There were some coal-pit hills in front of us and the Germans advanced over them in thousands. That was about eleven o'clock in the morning, and the firing began in real earnest again.

The Germans by this time were full of furious hope and reckless courage, because they believed that they had got us on the run and that it was merely a question of hours before we were wiped out of their way. Their blood was properly up, and so was ours, and I think we were a great deal hotter than they were, though we were heavily outnumbered. We hadn't the same opinion of German soldiers that the Germans had, and as they rushed on towards us we opened a fire from the trenches that simply destroyed them.

Some brave deeds were done and some awful sights were seen on the top of the coal-pits. A company of Germans were on one of the tops and an officer and about a dozen men of the "Koylis" went round one side of the pit and tried to get at them. Just as they reached the back of the pit the German artillery opened fire on the lot, Germans and all—that was one of their tricks. They would rather sacrifice some of their own men themselves than let any of ours escape—and they lost many in settling their account with the handful of Englishmen who had rushed behind the pit at a whole company of Germans.

Hereabouts, at the pits, the machine-gun fire on both sides was particularly deadly. Lieutenant Pepys, who was in charge of the machine-gun of our section, was killed by shots from German machine-guns, and when we went away we picked him up and carried him with us on the machine-gun limber until we buried him outside a little village in a colliery district.

He was a very nice gentleman and the first officer to go down. When he fell Lieutenant N. B. Dennison, the brigade machine-gun officer, took charge. He volunteered to take over the gun, and was either killed or wounded. Then Lieutenant Unett, the well-known gentleman jockey, crawled on his stomach to the first line of the trenches, with some men, dragging a machine-gun behind them. They got this gun into the very front of the line of the trenches, then opened fire on the Germans with disastrous effect. Lieutenant Unett was wounded and lay in the open all the time.

This gallant deed was done between twelve noon and one o'clock, and I was one of the few men who saw it. I am glad to be able to pay my humble tribute to it.

There was a battery of the Royal Field Artillery on our left rear, about 800 yards behind the front line of trenches. Our gunners had such excellent range on the Germans that the German gunners were finding them with high explosive shell. It was mostly those shells that were dropping on them till they got the range and killed the gunners. There were only about five who were not either killed or wounded. The officer was wounded; but in spite of that he carried a wounded man round the bottom of the hill, then went back and fetched another man and repeated the journey until he had taken every one of the five away. After that he returned, picked up a spade and smashed the sights of the gun and made it useless. We heard some time afterwards that he had been killed.

This brave deed was witnessed by most of us who were in the front line of trenches.

When the German guns were got into position in front of us and the Germans tried their hardest to blow us out of our trenches, they searched for our artillery and, failing to discover it, they grew more determined than ever to rout us out of the place from which we were doing deadly damage.

In spite of the heavy losses around us we held on, and all the more stubbornly because we expected every moment that the French would come up and reinforce us. The French were due about four o'clock, but owing to some accident they did not arrive, and it seemed as if nothing could save us.

There was a falling off in our artillery fire, and it was clear that one of our batteries had been put out of action. And no wonder, for the German guns were simply raining shells upon us. The Germans at that time were sticking to the dense formations which had been their practice since the war began—and they hurled themselves forward in clouds towards the 37th Field Battery.

So furiously did they rush, so vast were their numbers, and so certain were they that they had the guns as good as captured, that they actually got within a hundred yards of the battery.

It was at this terrible crisis that Captain Douglas Reynolds and volunteers rushed up with two teams and limbered up two guns, and in spite of all the German batteries and rifles did one gun was saved. This was a wonderful escape, in view of the nearness of the German infantry and their numbers, and for their share in the desperate affair the captain and two of the drivers—Drane and Luke—who had volunteered, got the Victoria Cross.

In a way we had got used to retiring, and we were not at the end of it even now, by a good deal, for on our left the Borderers were withdrawing and on our right the Manchesters were being forced right back; fighting magnificently and leaving the ground littered with their dead and wounded.

The Yorkshire Light Infantry were left in the centre of the very front line of the trenches, where we were heavily pressed. We made every mortal effort to hold our ground, and C Company was ordered up from the second line to reinforce us in the first.

Imagine what it meant for a company of infantry to get from one trench to another at a time like that, to leave shelter, to rush across a space of open ground that was literally riddled with shrapnel and rifle bullets, and in the daytime, too, with the Germans in overwhelming force at point-blank range.

But the order had been given, and C Company obeyed. The men sprang from their trench, they rushed across a fire-swept zone—and the handful of them who were not shot down made a final dash and simply tumbled into our trench and strengthened us. They had just about lost their first wind, but were soon hard at it again with the rifle and did murderous work, if only to get something back on account of the comrades who had fallen.

It was a help, a big help, to have C Company with us in the front trench; but even with this reinforcement we could do nothing, and after we had made a hot stand the order came to retire. That was about half-past four in the afternoon.

Things had been bad before; they were almost hopeless now, for to retire meant to show ourselves in the open and become targets for the German infantry; but our sole chance of salvation was to hurry away—there was no thought of surrender.

When the order was given there was only one thing to do—jump out of the trenches and make a rush, and we did both; but as soon as we were seen a storm of bullets struck down most of the men.

At such a time it is every man for himself, and it is hardly possible to think of anything except your own skin. All I wanted to do was to obey orders and get out of the trench and away from it.

I had rushed about half-a-dozen yards when I felt a curious tug at my boot. I looked to see what was the matter and found that my foot had been clutched by a poor chap who was wounded and was lying on the ground unable to move.

"For God's sake, save me!" he cried, and before I knew what was happening I had got hold of him and slung him across my back. I can't pretend to tell you details of how it was all done, because I don't clearly remember. There was no time to think of much besides the bullets and the fastest way of getting out of their reach. Rain was falling, not heavily, but it was drizzling, and this made the ground greasy and pretty hard going.

I had not gone far before the poor chap complained that my equipment hurt him and begged me to get it out of his way. The only thing to be done was to drop the equipment altogether, so I halted and somehow got the pack and the rest of it off, and I let my rifle go, too, for the weight of the lot, with the weight of a man, was more than I could tackle.

I picked my man up again, and had struggled on for twenty or thirty yards when I had to stop for a rest.

Just then I saw the major of the company, who said, "What's the matter with him?"

I could not speak, so I pointed to the man's knees, which were shot with shrapnel; then the major answered, "All right! Take him as far as you can, and I hope you'll get him safely out of it."

I picked him up again and off I went, making straight over the hill at the back of the position we had taken, so that he should be safe from the German fire. The point I wanted to reach was about a mile away, and it was a dreadful journey; but I managed to do it, and when I had got there, after many rests, I started to carry my man to the nearest village, which was some distance off.

I got to the village, but the German heavy shells were dropping so fast that I could not stay there, and they told me to carry him into the next village. I was pretty well worn out by this time, but I started again, and at last with a thankful heart I reached the village and got the man into a house where wounded men were being put.

How far did I carry him?

Well, it was calculated that the distance was three miles; but I never felt the weight. Yes, he was quite conscious and kept on moaning and saying, "Oh!" and telling me that if ever he got out of it he would remember me; but I said that he mustn't talk such nonsense—for I wanted him to stop thanking me and to keep his spirits up.

I don't know how long I was in getting him over the ground, for I had no idea of time.

Having put my man in safety I left the house and began to go back to the position, expecting to find some of the regiments to rejoin, but when I reached the firing line there were no regiments left. They had been forced to retire, and the ground was covered with the dead and wounded, as it was impossible to bring all the wounded away.

There was a road at this particular point, and on reaching the top of it I saw the Germans advancing, about 500 yards away. Between them and myself there was a field-gun, with the horses hooked in, ready to move off; but I saw that there was only a wounded trumpeter with it.

I rushed up to him and shouted, "What's wrong?"

"I'm hurt," he said. "The gun has to be got away; but there's nobody left to take it."

I looked all around, and saw that there were no English gunners left— there were only the Germans swarming up, 500 yards away and badly wanting to get at the gun.

There was not a second to lose. "Come on," I said, and with that I hoisted the trumpeter into the saddle of the near wheel horse, and clambering myself into the saddle of the lead horse we got the gun going and made a dash up the hill.

"I hoisted the trumpeter into the saddle."

There was only the one road, and this was so littered up and fenced about with wire entanglements that we could not hope to escape by it. Our only chance was by dashing at the hill, and this we did—and a terrible business it was, because we were forced to gallop the gun over the dead bodies of our own men—mostly artillerymen, they were. Many of the poor chaps had crawled away from their battery and had died on the hillside or on the road.

We carried on over the hill, and when the Germans saw what we were doing they rained shells and bullets on us. One or two of the horses were hit, and a bullet knocked my cap off and took a piece of skin from my head—just here. But that didn't hurt me much, nor did another bullet which went through my coat. We carried on, and got over the hill, just driving straight ahead, for we couldn't steer, not even to avoid the dead.

I daresay the bullet that carried off my cap stunned me a bit, at any rate I didn't remember very much after that, for the time being; all I know is that we galloped madly along, and dashed through two or three villages. There was no one in the first village; but in the second I saw an old lady sitting outside a house, with two buckets of water, from which soldiers were drinking. She was rocking to and fro, with her head between her hands, a pitiful sight. Shells were dropping all around and the place was a wreck.

I carried on at full stretch for about ten miles, tearing along to get to the rear of the column. I don't remember that I ever looked back; but I took it that the trumpeter was still in the saddle of the wheel horse.

At last I caught up with the column; then I looked round for the trumpeter, but he was not there, and I did not know what had become of him. That was the first I knew of the fact that I had been driving the gun by myself.

Willy-nilly I had become a sort of artilleryman, and from that time until the 28th I attached myself to the guns; but on that day I rejoined what was left of my old regiment.

I had been in charge of twelve men, but when I inquired about them I found that only three were left—nine had been either killed or wounded, and the rest of the battalion had suffered in proportion. That gives some idea of the desperate nature of the fighting and the way in which the little British army suffered during the first three days after Mons.

The officer who had seen me carrying the man off did not see me go back, but a sergeant who knew me noticed me passing through the village with the gun and he was the first man of my battalion that I saw. This was Sergeant Marchant, who, for his gallantry in helping another sergeant, who was wounded, was awarded the Distinguished Conduct Medal. In that fine affair he was helped by Company-Sergeant-Major Bolton, and both of them were mentioned in despatches.

Of course I never thought of saying anything about what I had done; but I was sent for and asked if it was true, and I said I had got the man away and helped to take the gun off, and this was confirmed by the major who had seen me carrying the man.

For the day's work at Le Cateau two Victoria Crosses were given to my regiment—one to Major C. A. L. Yate, "Cal," he was called, because of his initials, and one to myself.

Major Yate was a very fine officer. He joined us and took command of B Company just before we went out to the war. On this day he was in the trenches, on our left rear, not very far from where I was. When we went into action he had 220 men, but they caught so much of the hot fire which was meant for the battery behind that he lost all his men except nineteen when he was surrounded and captured. The day before this happened the major declared that if it came to a pinch and they were surrounded he would not surrender—and he did not surrender now. Reckless of the odds against him he headed his nineteen men in a charge against the Germans—and when that charge was over only three of the company could be formed up. All the rest of B Company were either killed or wounded or taken prisoners, though very few prisoners were taken. The major was one of them; but he was so badly wounded that he lived only a very short time, and died as a prisoner of war. His is one of the cases in which the Cross is given although the winner of it is dead. Major Yate was an absolute gentleman and a great favourite with us all. He had had a lot of experience in the Far East and at home, and I am sure that if he had lived he would have become a general. He was always in front, and his constant cry was "Follow me!"

From Le Cateau we got to the Valley of the Aisne and were in trenches for ten days. At midnight on September 24th we advanced two miles beyond the river, which we had crossed by pontoons because all the other bridges had been blown up.

We reached a little village and stayed there in shelters underneath the houses, where all the inhabitants slept. We stayed in one of these cellars and went on outpost at four in the morning and came off at four next morning, then went on again at four a.m.

We were only 250 yards from the Germans, who were in a small wood outside the village, opposite the houses. They had snipers out and were sniping at us all the time. We barricaded the windows of the houses and knocked bricks out of the walls to make loopholes, and through these loopholes we sniped the Germans, and they did their level best to pick us off too. Every time your head was shown a dozen bullets came, and you could not see where they came from. Two or three of our men were killed by snipers; but there was no real chance of getting to grips, for there was barbed wire everywhere, and nothing could be done till this was cut. Night was the only time when the wire could be cut—and night work was both eerie and nerve-racking.

We had "listeners" to listen for any movement by the enemy. A sentry in peace times means a man who walks up and down, smartly dressed, but in war time, at night, he is a listener, and in the daytime he is a "watcher"—he can see in the daytime and hear at night. That is one of the little things which show how greatly war changes the customs of peace.

It was outside Béthune, when we were in reserve to the rest of the brigade, that I was wounded. We had got well into October and we were behind trenches, with French infantry on our right. At night we advanced, on a level with the firing line, and in the darkness we dug trenches. We were then next to the King's Own Scottish Borderers. We finished the trenches before the early hours of the morning and stuck in them till five in the afternoon, when we heard some shouts, and on looking over we saw that the Germans were making a charge.

We opened rapid fire and the Germans answered very smartly, having dropped down. But they were not down long, for up they sprang and with further shouts on they came and got within three hundred yards of us. Then we were ordered to fix bayonets and be ready to charge at any moment; but before we started charging we rushed into another line of trenches in front of us, and there we mixed with the Borderers.

This fight in the night was a thrilling affair, the chief guide on each side being the flashes of the rifles, and these were incessant. The Germans were firing rapidly at anything they could see; but there was little to see except the tiny forks of flame. They must have heard us, however, and that, of course, would help them. One strange thing happened when we reached the trench, and that was that we had to wake up some of the men. In spite of the fighting they were sleeping—but war turns everything upside down, and the British soldier reaches a point when it takes a lot to disturb him.

Suddenly, at this crisis, I felt as if my leg had been struck by something that vibrated, like a springboard, and I dropped down. I was dizzy, but did not think I was hit, and I supposed that if I stayed down for a few minutes I should be all right and able to go on. So I sat down, but quickly found that I could not move, and on feeling my leg I discovered that it was wet and warm, and I knew what that meant, so I took off my equipment and put it down and began to crawl back to the trench I had left when we charged.

I crawled across a mangel-wurzel field to a house of some sort, then I must have become unconscious, for the next thing I knew was that I was being carried along on a stretcher.

It was only yesterday that a friend in my battalion wrote to tell me that we were crawling pretty close together through the mangel-wurzel field. He was shot in the arm and stopped two of the Borderers' stretcher-bearers just in time to have me put on a stretcher.

I had a natural walking-stick which I had cut from a vine, and of which I was very fond. I had fastened it to my rifle and was so proud of it that I said I would carry it through the war, if I could. My friend must have known how I prized the vine-stick, for when he was sent home he brought it with him, and it's waiting for me when I leave hospital.

I also had a letter from my company officer a few days ago. He says he missed me that night, but he could not make out what had happened. He heard that a complete set of equipment had been found, and on learning that I was wounded he assumed that it was mine, and that I had been carried away and left it. He told me that on the very night I was wounded they were relieved by the French infantry, and that he himself was hit ten days afterwards. It was the day before I was wounded that I heard that I was recommended for the French Military Medal, and that was as big a surprise to me as the news that I had been given the Victoria Cross.

That equipment of mine had a tragic history. During the first day of the Aisne I was without equipment and set to work to get some. A bugler of my battalion had been killed by shrapnel and I was told by my officer to go and get his equipment. "Treat him gently, poor chap," said the officer, and you may be sure I did. I helped myself, and thinking that the poor lad's mother might like a memento I brought away his "iron-rations" tin. This is riddled with bullet-holes, just as the bugler was.

There is one thing more that I would like to say, and it is about my birthday, which falls on September 7th. As I had left the colours and gone into the Reserve I thought I could look forward to a fine celebration of the anniversary. And there *was* a fine celebration, too, for on September 7th our retiring before the Germans ended and we started to advance and drive them back.

Could any British soldier want a finer birthday celebration than that?

A rougher recreation of an Allied trench made for the WW1 centenary - Image: John M

Chapter VI - British Fighters in French Wars

Private J. Boyers, Durham Light Infantry.

[We very slowly learned something of the many extraordinary features of this amazing war. Nothing is too astonishing or stupendous to happen in connection with the fight to crush the militarism of Prussia. Through this story by Private J. Boyers, of the Durham Light Infantry—the old 68th Foot, long known by reason of its devotion on many a bloody field like Salamanca and Inkerman as the "Faithful Durhams"—we get to know something of the British and French fighting side by side in the forts at Lille, one of the strongest of the famous fortresses of France. Lille is a great manufacturing town, the Manchester of France, and early in October 1914, and later, it was the scene of much desperate fighting between the Allied Armies and the Germans.\]

I WENT from England with the first party in the Expeditionary Force, and after landing on the other side of the Channel, we had a march of fifty miles to Mons, where I had my first battle.

I was in the great retirement—but I suppose you have heard enough about that and Mons already, so I will leave it. After that beginning, I took part in the Battle of the Marne and the Battle of the Aisne, and later on I was shot in the thigh and bowled out.

I am only a young soldier—I am a native of Sunderland, and was born in 1891—and I have only been in the army a few months—in the old 68th, the "Faithful Durhams," so I think I have seen a fair lot of the big war and have got to know what it means.

The Durhams have done splendidly and suffered terribly, and many a chum of mine is sleeping with thousands more British soldiers on the battlefields of France and Belgium. A great many have been wounded, and of course there are a number of missing, mostly men, I dare say, who are prisoners of war.

I had been at sea before joining the army, and thought I knew something about roughing it; but even the North Sea in bad weather was nothing compared with the hardships of the retirement from Mons, and the living and sleeping in the trenches when the ground was sodden and deep in water.

Sometimes we were very short of food, and once for several days on end we were almost starving, because the supplies could not get up to us, and we had been forced to throw away a lot of our packs and things.

A good many of us had to carry a seven-pound tin of bully beef in addition to our heavy packs and a great many rounds of ammunition. In the fearfully hot weather we could not carry all this weight, and the tins of beef had to go. We should have been thankful for them later on, when we ran short and some of the beef we had with us had gone bad through the tins getting punctured, which happened in all sorts of strange ways, including bullet-holes and bayonet pricks. But these were things that couldn't be helped, and in spite of them all we kept very cheerful, and often enough, both on the march and in the trenches and French forts, when we got to them, we sang and joked and whistled as if there was no such thing going on as war.

Our officers shared everything with us, and suffered just as we did, though often worse, so that whenever we got a bit downhearted, their example cheered us up and put us right. I don't think there's a man who's fought in this great war who won't say the same thing about his officers.

We had so much fierce fighting when the work really began, and saw so many strange and dreadful things, that it is not easy to say what stands out most clearly in our minds in such a business, but one of the things I do remember, and shall never forget, is the week or so we spent in one of the big French forts at Lille, fighting side by side with French soldiers. I will tell you about that later, but we did a lot before we got to Lille.

When we were on the march we had a great deal of exciting work to do in hunting Germans. Small bodies of them were everywhere, apart from the immense numbers of spies who were in the Lille district and elsewhere.

The French bagged a lot of spies and gave them short shrift. They hid in all sorts of queer places—some of them got into the tall mill chimneys—but they were routed out and shot.

We found a fair lot of Germans in houses and farms when we were on the march. We examined these places thoroughly. When we arrived at farmhouses and suchlike places, a non-commissioned officer, with a small party of men would make inquiries, often with the help of French cavalrymen who were with us and could speak English, and we always found that threats of fearful punishment to the womenfolk had been made by the Germans if they told us that any Germans had been seen about. But the women told us readily enough, especially when there happened to be any Germans in hiding—those who were too drunk to get away and had been left behind. It didn't take long to make these fellows prisoners, and they rubbed their eyes a lot when they got sober and found that the British had bagged them—though I fancy that most of them were glad to be caught and out of the fighting.

We saw some dreadful sights in these farms and houses that we entered, and it was no uncommon thing for us to bury the women who had been done to death by these invaders who were worse than heathens. We had to carry out this sad work at night, to escape the German fire, for no matter what we were doing they went for us with rifles and machine-guns and anything else that came handy.

Time after time on the march we saw proof of the terrible way in which the French and Germans fought, and saw how bravely the French had defended their country and how freely they had given their lives to get something like even with the enemy.

The Frenchmen were naturally even more upset than the British soldiers were at many of the sights that met us, and in the streets along which we marched we often saw dead bodies of Frenchmen and Germans lying close together, where they had fallen after a desperate fight on the pavements or in the roadway. They had met and fought to the death, and it looked as if no quarter had been given. And with all this there had been a perfectly savage destruction of everything that the Germans could lay their hands on.

The Germans had thieved and killed wherever they had gone, led on in the work by their officers, and little supposing, I fancy, that the day of reckoning had come for them and that their brutal game was being spoiled. There is no doubt that they had been taught that they were going to have a walk over in France and were going to have a good time in Paris; but some of them were poor enough specimens when we caught them or they surrendered.

After the terrific battles of the Marne and the Aisne we were transferred rather quickly to La Bassée, which is not far from Lille, and then we had to take a share in defending Lille, in one of the big forts just outside the town.

The Germans had got up into that part of the country in very strong force, and they were making furious efforts to smash the forts and get hold of Lille, which had become a most important place for them.

Lille is a large manufacturing town and was very strongly defended by forts and in other ways. These big forts, about half-a-dozen in number, form a ring round the town and command all the countryside, or rather did, for they have been pretty badly hammered by this time; while the town itself is protected in other ways. Lille was also one of the big centres for French troops, but owing to the heavy drain caused by the immense numbers of Germans that had to be dealt with at the Aisne there were not a great many first-rate troops left, and a good deal of the defence had to fall on the territorials.

The particular fort where I had my strangest experiences was about a mile from Lille, and from the outside it looked like a low hill-top, so much so that when we were getting near it the fort seemed like a little round hill rising from the plain.

The fort was built of immense blocks of stone, and, as far as one could tell, great quantities of steel, so that its strength must have been enormous.

It was a romantic sort of business to get into the fort, because, first of all, we had to pass the sentries, then some huge stone sliding doors were opened, by a lever, I suppose, in the same way as the midway doors of a District Railway carriage open and shut. They were very big and heavy doors, yet they opened and shut quite easily, and when they were closed you could hardly see a crack between them.

Past this gloomy entrance was a narrow walled slope which led into darkness. We went down the slope into what looked like an archway and then we got into proper blackness. It was some time before you could get used to such darkness, but at last I saw that we had reached a large vault; but I can't pretend to give details, because I never had a chance of properly making them out, and we were more concerned about the Germans than we were about the fort.

Of course it can be easily understood that owing to the presence of great quantities of ammunition and inflammable stores, only the dimmest lighting was possible—in fact, there was practically no lighting at all except by little portable electric lamps, and as for smoking, that was absolutely off.

The instant we reached the fort we were told that smoking was most strictly forbidden, and that disobedience was punishable by death. The French soldier is as fond as the British Tommy of his smoke, but it is a remarkable thing that in the darkness of the fort we didn't feel the want of smoking, which isn't much of a catch in the pitch darkness. As a matter of fact I had no wish to smoke when we were in the fort, so I was never tempted to run the risk of being shot.

Cooking, like smoking, was out of the question, for you can no more smoke with safety in a magazine like that than you can in a coal-mine—a spark is enough to do tremendous mischief, let alone a fire; so our rations had to be brought to us by the Army Service Corps, though they, with their carts, were a long way off.

The A.S.C. chaps were splendid all through, and the men in the fighting line owe a lot to them.

In this black dungeon, with such cunning Germans about, a sentry's challenge was a good deal more than a formality; but it nearly became one when the welcome commissariat man arrived. But for his coming we should have had to fall back on our emergency rations. These were good, of their kind, but they can't compare with the best efforts of the A.S.C.

But I'm getting off the track a bit. In the side of the vault, or cavern, there was a low, shallow dug-out which was meant to hold a rifleman lying at full stretch. This was something like a small cubicle in size and shape, and to enter it in the darkness was a proper problem. After a try or two, however, you got into the way of stumbling comfortably into it. By crouching and creeping, and using your hands and knees, you could secure a position from which it was fairly easy to draw yourself up into the dug-out. I dwell on this because I think it is important, seeing that four of us took two-hour watches throughout the twenty-four hours, so that getting to and from such a dug-out becomes an event in your daily life.

At one end of the dug-out was a loophole for a rifle or a maxim-gun, and here we patiently waited for those pests, the snipers. These German potters gave us no rest; but many a German who thought he was well hidden got the finishing touch from one of our loopholes.

This was thrilling fighting, especially when things became hot, and we manned all the loopholes in the fort, to the number of four, and at a pinch we could use two maxims at each. There were fourteen of us in the fort altogether, four officers and ten men. The orders, being in French, sounded very strange at first, but to my surprise, I soon fell into the way of understanding what was said around me, certainly so far as ordinary little things were concerned. I shall never forget the French for water so long as I remember the thirst I had in the black depths of the fort.

The life in the fort was one of the strangest parts of the whole of the fighting. It was queer enough to be in France, fighting with the French, but a good deal queerer to be living in one of the big famous French forts which the Germans were trying to pound to bits with their enormous siege guns. But we soon settled down and got fairly well used to the sound of the fort's guns and the row of the German artillery and the crashing of the shells around us.

We were told off into parties in the fort, each party being commanded by a non-commissioned officer, who used to light the way for us with an electric lamp that he carried in front of him, hung round his neck.

We ate and drank and slept with the French gunners, and taken altogether we were very comfortable, and were spared something of the awful noise of the firing, for when the guns of the forts were fired the noise was worse than thunderbolts, and everything about was shaken in the most extraordinary manner.

The Germans were mad to get at us and they shot tons and tons of shells at us, and time after time made efforts to storm the forts and Lille itself. In these attempts they lost immense numbers of men, and when we got outside of the fort we saw the dead bodies of the Germans lying about in thousands—so thick on the ground were they that we had to clamber over them as best we could.

Our own fort was pretty lucky, but the next one to us was very badly damaged, huge holes being made where the monster shells got home, and most of the defenders of the fort being wiped out. The German big guns certainly did a vast amount of mischief against forts—so the Germans will know what to expect when our own big guns get to work on forts in Germany.

It was soon clear that it would not be possible to hold on at Lille for long, because we were so hopelessly outnumbered. The fight went on, day and night, for a full week, and the Germans bombarded everything.

On Sunday, October 4th, there was some desperate fighting in the streets of the town and the outskirts. German troops were rushed up in armoured trains and motors, but when it came to hand-to-hand fighting they were not much good, and on the Monday they were driven away with heavy loss.

We had a few goes at them with the bayonet, and that charging was very hard work. It had to be done in short rushes of about a hundred yards, but we could not get near enough to them to give the bayonet a fair chance. In that respect it was the same old story—the Germans would not face the steel. In anything like equal numbers they can't stand up against a charge. They would mostly run for it, firing at us over their shoulders as they bolted, but not doing a great deal of mischief that way. When they could run no more and saw that the game was up, they would throw away their rifles and surrender, and we then brought them in.

Before the fighting began, and while it was going on, a good many of the inhabitants got into a panic and fled to Boulogne and Calais; but the French troops held out gamely, and on the Tuesday a fearful lot of execution was done amongst the masses of Germans by the French artillery fire. Neither the German guns nor the infantry could make a stand against this onslaught, and at this time the German losses were particularly heavy, hundreds of men falling together. At the end of that part of the battle the Germans for the time being were completely routed, and they were driven back a good dozen miles.

The Durhams suffered greatly in the fighting, and the good old West Yorkshires, who had seen a lot of hard work with us, had been badly cut up too. Some splendid help was given by the little Gurkhas, who had joined the British; but unfortunately I was not able to see much of what they did, because soon after they appeared with their famous knives I got my wound.

Some of the most exciting and dangerous work was done at night, when we tried to get at the Germans with the bayonet and rout them out of their trenches and positions. We had to do everything so quietly—creep out of the forts, creep along the ground, and creep up to the enemy as near as we could get, and sometimes that was not very close, because of such things as barbed wire entanglements.

These entanglements were particularly horrible, because they were so hard to overcome and tore the flesh and clothing. At first we had a pretty good way of destroying them, and that was by putting the muzzles of our rifles on the wire and blowing it away; but there were two serious drawbacks to that trick—one was that it was a waste of ammunition, and the other was that the noise of the firing gave us away, and let the Germans loose on us with guns and rifles.

We soon got too canny to go on with that practice, and just before I was wounded and sent home a very ingenious arrangement had been fixed to the muzzle of the rifle for wire-cutting—a pair of shears which you could work with a swivel from near the trigger, so that instead of putting the muzzle of the rifle against the wire, you could cut it by using the pliers.

It was in one of these night affairs that I was nearly finished as a soldier. I was ordered to join a reconnoitring party. We got clear of the fort, and made our way over the country for about a mile. We were then in a field which had been harvested and harrowed, so that it was pretty hard ground to go over. In spite of it all we were getting on very nicely when the Germans got wind of our movements and opened a terrible fire with rifles and maxims.

We lost a lot of men, and where a man fell there he had to lie, dead or living.

Suddenly I fell plump on the ground, and found that I could not get up again, though I did my best to keep up with my chums. Then I felt an awful pain in my thigh and knew that I was hurt, but I must have been struck five minutes before I fell, by a bullet from a German rifle. It had gone clean through my right thigh. They told me afterwards that I had had a very narrow shave indeed; but a miss is as good as a mile.

I knew there was nothing for it but pluck and patience, so I made the best of things, and waited till the day broke and brought the battalion stretcher-bearers, who always came out just about dawn to collect the wounded.

"We found a fair lot of Germans in houses and farms."

I was lying on the ground, in a sort of ditch, for six hours before I was picked up by the stretcher-bearers and carried to a stable which was being used as a temporary hospital.

The Germans fired on the wounded as they were being carried off in the grey light, but they didn't hit me again.

I lay in the stable for about eight hours, waiting for the ambulance, which took me to the rail-head, and then I was put in a train and taken to Rouen— and that travelling was simply awful, because the French trains jolt like traction-engines.

All the same, I had a pleasant voyage to Southampton, and hoped that I might be sent to a hospital near home, but I was too ill to go a long journey to the north, so I was taken to Woolwich, and afterwards sent here, to the Royal Hospital at Richmond, where everybody is kindness itself, and can't do enough for you, it seems.

I've had a month in bed, so far, but I'm hoping to be out of it soon and hobbling about.

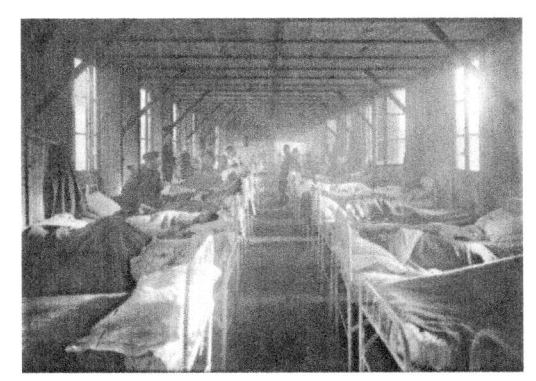

A ward of wounded soldiers during World War One – this is a purpose-built 'Base Hospital' situated in France

Chapter VII – German Treachery and Hatred

Corporal W. Bratby, Middlesex Regiment.

[*"Die hard, my men, die hard!" shouted the heroic Colonel Inglis, when, at Albuhera, in the Peninsular War, his regiment, the 57th Foot, were furiously engaged with the enemy. And the regiment obeyed, for when the bloody fight was ended twenty-two out of twenty-five officers had been killed or wounded, 425 of 570 rank and file had fallen and thirty bullets had riddled the King's Colour. The 57th is now the 1st Battalion Middlesex Regiment, but the regiment is still best known by its gallant nickname of the "Die-Hards." It has suffered exceptional losses in this war, and the story of some of its doings is told by Corporal W. Bratby, who relates a tale which he has described as a brother's revenge.*]

THE old "Die-Hards" went into action at Mons nearly a thousand strong; but when, after Mons had been left behind, a roaring furnace, the roll was called, not more than 270 of us were left. D Company came out a shattered remnant—only thirty-six men, and no officers. When what was left of us marched away, other regiments were shouting, "Three cheers for the Die-Hards!" And three rousing cheers they gave; but I had no heart for them, because I had left my younger brother Jack, a "Die-Hard" like myself. They told me that he had been killed by a bursting shell while doing his duty with the machine-gun section.

I did not say much. I asked the adjutant if any of the machine-gun section had returned, and he answered sadly, "No, they've all gone."

Jack and I were brothers and had been good old chums all our lives—I had taught him a bit of boxing and he was most promising with the gloves, and we had a widowed mother to keep; so I really felt as if something had gone snap in my head and that all I cared for was to get my revenge from the Germans. The last words I heard him say were, "Well, Bill, I'm going right into the firing line," and I remember laughing and saying, "Yes, Jack, but you're not the only one who's going to do that."

Jack laughed too and said, "All right, Bill, I'll see you in the firing line," and with that he went and I saw no more of him.

I had been in the regiment five years and nine months when the war broke out and Jack had served more than two years. I had become a corporal and he was a lance-corporal.

The days in the beginning were swelteringly hot; but the "Die-Hards," being typical Cockneys, made the best of them. Our Brigade consisted of ourselves (the 4th Middlesex), the 2nd Royal Scots, the 1st Gordon Highlanders and the 2nd Royal Irish Rifles. We began operations with trench digging, one particular trench, the machine-gun trench, being allotted to B Company. I helped to superintend the construction of the trenches, and I was proud of the work when I saw what was done from them when the Germans showed themselves.

Our machine-gun caused enormous havoc amongst the German ranks, and I am sure that my brother did his part in settling a lot of them, for he was keen on his work and full of go. The Royal Irish at this stage were doing splendidly—they were not more than 350 yards from the enemy, separated from them by a railway—and they were lucky enough to fetch one gun out of action again, but the enormously superior numbers of the Germans told and the famous retreat began. The machine-gunners had suffered very heavily and it was hard to learn anything definite about the position in the trenches.

Officers and men were falling everywhere on both sides, and I saw a reconnoitring patrol of Uhlans bowled over in trying to avoid some of the 4th Royal Fusiliers. An officer and seven men of the Uhlans were killed in that little affair without getting in a shot in return. It was not much, but it was something cheering after what we had gone through at Mons. We looked upon it as a bit of sport, and after that we went into châteaux, cafés and other places, and discussed affairs in a proper Tommy-like spirit. It is very strange, but if it had not been for the language I could have thought at times that I was back in Kilburn or in London, on strike duty again, as I was at the time of the railway trouble three years ago.

We were fighting a rearguard action for three days right off the reel, and doing that wonderful march to which "Kitchener's test" or anything like it was a mere nothing. Owing to the heat, we discarded overcoats, kits and in some cases rifles and equipment. Our transport was blown to pieces three days after Mons, which to the 8th Brigade is known as *the* Wednesday.

But lost kit and shattered transport mattered little to most of us, and certainly had slight significance for me, because the only thing I had in mind was this determination to get revenge. I am not exaggerating in the least, I am merely putting down on record the state of my feelings and wishing to make you understand how remarkable a change had come over me, an alteration such as is brought about, I take it, by war, and war alone. Perhaps, too, the excessive stress and strain of those early days of the war had something to do with my condition; but whatever the cause, there it was. Danger itself meant nothing, and I, like the rest of us, took the ordinary fighting and the incessant and truly horrible shell fire as a matter of course, a part of the day's work. I bided my time, and it came.

We had crossed the Aisne, a dangerous unit still, in spite of our losses, for we had received reinforcements from the base; but just before crossing the river we sat down on the road, waiting for a favourable opportunity to cross by a pontoon bridge which the Engineers were building. That pontoon replaced a bridge which had been blown up.

On the word "Rise" we fell in, and in doing so a man had the misfortune to shoot himself through the hand.

The colonel came up at once and ordered the injured man to go back to the hospital in a village about a mile and a half up the road, in rear of the bridge. I was told off to take him, and we went to a house that had been turned into a hospital, the people in it being typically French. There were some sad cases there, amongst them one of our own fellows who had been severely wounded and a trooper of the 4th Hussars who was the only survivor of a reconnoitring party. He had been shot while going through the village that morning. Just at that time we had had many losses of small bodies—in one case a sergeant and five men had been blown to pieces.

After I had got the wounded man into the hospital I asked the "monsieur" in charge of the house for some tea, which he very willingly produced—it had no milk in it, of course, but by that time I had almost forgotten that milk existed.

At this time the village was being shelled, but that did not affect the enjoyment of my tea-drinking, and after that refreshing draught and a chunk of "bully" and some biscuit crumbs which I found in the corner of a none-too-clean haversack, I "packed down" for the night.

At about four o'clock next morning I awoke and went back to the bridge, which my battalion had crossed on the previous day, the "Die-hards" being the first to have the honour to cross. By this time we had got past the sweltering stage of things and had become accustomed to soaking weather, and on this particular morning I was thoroughly cold and wet and generally "fed up" with things; but I still glowed with the longing to get level with the Germans.

You must bear in mind that regiments had been broken up and scattered in the most astonishing manner and had become mixed up with other regiments, and I had lost my own and had to set to work to find it.

I got over the bridge and reached some artillery.

"Have you seen anything of the Middlesex?" I asked.

"Yes," the gunners answered, "they've just gone into action on the brow of the hill."

I made my way towards the top of a neighbouring hill and found that my battalion had taken up a position there, but I had to wander about aimlessly, and I did so till I came across one or two men who were separated from the battalion. They directed me to the actual position, which was on the ridge of the hill, and to the ridge I went and found that it was lined with remnants of the brigade.

I tried to find my own company, but could not do so, as it had been surprised in the night; so I attached myself to another and lay down with the corporal on the sodden ground.

Wet through, cold, hungry and physically miserable, but still tough in spirit, we lay there, wishing that all sorts of impossible things would happen.

The corporal showed me where he had hit a German scout. We watched the poor devil rolling about—then we finished him off.

In addition to the wet there was a fog, and under cover of this the Germans crept up and were on us almost before we knew of their presence.

The alarm was first given by a man near us who was suffering from ague or some such ailment and had been moaning and groaning a good deal.

Suddenly he cried, "Here they are, corporal! Fire at 'em!"

My loaded rifle was lying just in front of me. I snatched it up, and as I did so the Germans jumped out of the mist on to us, with loud shouts. I brought the first German down and my chum dropped one; and we managed to fetch the officer down. He was carrying a revolver and a stick, like most German officers, so that you had no difficulty in distinguishing them.

When the alarm was given I gave a quick look over a small hump in the ground and then we were rushed; but I hated the idea of retiring, and kept on shouting, "Crawl back! Crawl back!"

Machine-guns and rifles were rattling and men were shouting and cursing. In the midst of it all I was sane enough to hang on to my fire till I got a good chance—and I did not wait for nothing.

Up came two Germans with a stretcher. They advanced till they were not more than twenty-five yards away, for I could see their faces quite clearly; then I took aim, and down went one of the pair and "bang" off the stretcher fell a maxim. The second German seemed to hesitate, but before he could pull himself together he had gone down too. I began to feel satisfied.

By this time the order to retire had been given and I kept on shouting, "Keep down! Crawl back!" and the lads crawled and jumped with curious laughs and curses.

In that excited retirement the man who was with me was shot in the chest. I halted for a little while to see what had really happened to him, and finding that he was killed I took his waterproof sheet and left him. I hurried on until I was in a valley, well away from the ridge; then an officer managed to get us together and lead us into a wood.

As we got into the wood I spotted a quarry. I said to the officer, "Is it best to go down here, sir?"

"I'll have a look—yes," he answered.

We went into the quarry, where there were Royal Scots, Middlesex, Gordons and Royal Irish.

The officer was afraid that we might be rushed, in which case we should be cut up, so he put a man out on scout. We were not rushed, however, and when the firing ceased we filed out and lined the ridge again, and there we lay, expecting the Germans to come back, but for the time being we saw no more of them.

By some means one of the Irishmen had got drunk and wanted to fight the Germans "on his own." He was shouting for them to come on and was wandering about. Soon afterwards he was found lying on the top of the hill, having been shot in the thigh. He was carried out of action and I have never heard of him since.

After that affair of the hill-crest we had a lot of trench work, and very harassing it was. For five days we stayed in trenches, so near to the enemy that it was death to show your head.

Trench fighting is one of the most terrible features of the war, for not only is there the constant peril of instant death, which, of course, every soldier gets accustomed to, but there is also the extreme discomfort and danger of illness arising from insanitary surroundings. Often enough, too, when a new trench was being dug we would find that we were working on ground that had been previously occupied, and the spades brought up many a ghastly reminder of an earlier fight.

Sometimes in this wonderful warfare we were so very close to the Germans that when we sang hymns—and many a hymn that a soldier has sung at his mother's knee has gone up from the trenches from many a brave lad who has given his life for his country—the Germans would harmonise with them. It was strange to hear these men singing like that and to bear in mind that they were the soldiers who had done such monstrous things as we saw during the retreat, when they thought that certain victory was theirs. Time after time, with my own eyes, I saw evidence of the brutal outrages of the German troops, especially on women and children, yet it seems hard to convince some of the people at home that these things have been done.

At one time in the trenches, for a whole week, we were so situated that we dare not even speak for fear of revealing our position—we were subjected to an enfilade fire and did not dare to speak or light a fire, which meant that we had no hot food for a week, and we could not even smoke, which was the biggest hardship of all for a lot of the lads. We were thankful when we were relieved; but were sorry indeed to find how dearly the newcomers paid for their experience. We had been cramped and uncomfortable, but pretty safe, and the Germans had not been able to get at us to do us any real mischief, but our reliefs walked about as unconcernedly as if they were on furlough, with the result that on the very first night they went into action they lost a hundred men.

The system of trenches grew into a sort of enormous gridiron, and if you walked about—which you could only attempt to do at night—you were almost certain to drop into a trench or a hole of some sort. This made getting about a very exciting job, and it added enormously to the intense strain of fighting in the trenches, a strain which was hardest to bear in the night-time, when we were constantly expecting attacks and when the Germans adopted all kinds of devices to get at us.

The Germans are what we call dirty fighters, and they will take advantage of anything to try and score over you. They have no respect for anything and made a particular point in many of the places they overran of desecrating the churches. They never hesitated to turn a place of worship into a scene for an orgy, and I remember going into one church after the Germans had occupied it and being shocked at their conduct. In this particular place they had been able to lay hands on a good deal of champagne and they had drunk to excess, turning the church into a drinking-place, so that when we reached it there was an indescribable scene—filthy straw on the floor, empty champagne bottles littered everywhere, and the whole building degraded and desecrated.

The Germans had got a French uniform and stuffed it with straw and propped it up to resemble a man, and on the uniform they had stuck a piece of paper with some writing on it in German. I do not know what the writing was, but I took it to be some insult to the brave men who were defending their country and preventing the Germans from getting anywhere near Paris. I could tell you much more and many things of the Germans' dirty fighting, and of things that were far worse than such an incident as turning a church into a drinking-place; but perhaps enough has been said on that point of late.

But that dirty fighting does not mean that the Germans do not fight bravely—far from it; they are hard cases, especially when they are in overwhelming numbers, which is the form of fighting that they like best of all.

They are great believers in weight and hurling masses of men at a given point, and they are absolutely mad at times when their opponents are the English.

I will tell you of a case which illustrates this particular hatred. One night we were attacked by the Germans, though there was but little hope of them doing anything serious, in view of the fact that we were in trenches and that there were the barbed wire entanglements everywhere. There had been no sign of an attack, but in the middle of the night a furious assault was made upon us and a young German by some extraordinary means managed to get through the entanglements. An officer of the Buffs was near us, and in some way which I cannot explain the German managed to reach him. With a fierce cry he sprang directly at the officer, put an arm round his neck, and with the revolver which he held in the other hand shot him.

It was the work of a moment; but it succeeded—so did our bayonet attack on the German, for almost as soon as his shot had rung out in the night a dozen bayonets had pierced him. He died very quickly, but not before he had managed to show how intensely he hated all the English. He was a fine young fellow, not more than seventeen or eighteen years old, and it was impossible not to admire the courage and cleverness he had shown in getting through the awful barbed wire entanglements and hurling himself upon us in the trenches in the middle of the night. The point that puzzles me even now, when I recall the incident, is how the young German managed to make such a clean jump for the officer. I daresay there was something more than luck in it.

At this time we were with the Buffs, who told us that they were being badly troubled by snipers. I was in a trench with Lieutenant Cole, who was afterwards killed, and he said to me, "Corporal, the snipers are worrying our people, but it's very difficult to locate them. Try and see what you can make out of it."

It was very difficult, but I set to work to try and make something out. Before long, with the help of the glasses, I concluded that the sniping came from a wood not far away, and I told the officer that I thought they were in a tree there. The consequence was that a platoon loaded up, went round, concentrated their fire on this particular spot and brought down two German roosters from a tree. We were glad to be rid of the pests, and they ought to have been satisfied, for they had had a very good innings.

I have been telling about the determination I had to be revenged for my brother's death. That was my great object, and I kept it in mind before anything else—and I think I carried it out. Apart from any motive, it is the British soldier's duty to do everything he can to settle the enemy, especially the Germans, and I am glad that I did my bit in this respect.

Now listen to what has really happened. After all that fighting and suffering with the grand old "Die-Hards" I got my own turn, after many wonderful escapes. A shell burst near me and the fragments peppered me on the right hand here and about this side of the body, and bowled me out for the time being. I was sent home, and here I am in London again, getting well and expecting the call to come at any time to go back to the front. When it comes I shall be ready to obey.

Look at this postcard. It is written, as you see, by a British soldier who is a prisoner of war in Germany, and it tells the glad news that my brother, who, I was told, was killed months ago by a bursting shell, is not dead, but is alive and well, although he is a prisoner of war.

Chapter VIII – Life in the Trenches

Private G. Townsend, 2nd Battalion East Lancashire Regiment.

[The winter of the war was marked by an abnormal rainfall and storms of uncommon severity: also by the extraordinary development of trench warfare. The rain and storms, the frost and snow, made it impossible to carry out the greater operations of campaigning, with the result that both sides dug themselves in and fought from rival trenches which in many cases were separated by only a few yards. This story deals with life in the trenches, at La Bassée, and it gives a wonderful understanding of the privations that have been uncomplainingly borne by British soldiers. The teller is Private G. Townsend, 2nd Battalion East Lancashire Regiment, who has had more than six years' service with the colours. These long-service men have compelled the attention of even the Germans who despised the "contemptible little army," for they have admitted that the seasoned British private soldier is the equal of a German non-commissioned officer.]

WHEN the rebellion broke out in South Africa we—the old "Lily Whites"—were the only imperial regiment kept in that country. We were sitting still and stiff for twenty days, till General Botha got his own troops ready. During that time we were guarding Cape Town, and it took us all we knew to hold in, because the big war was on, and we were about seven thousand miles away from the seat of it. We had to wait till General Botha was ready, and that was not for more than a month after the British and the Germans met in Belgium.

We were eager to get away from South Africa, and at last we sailed—but what a slow voyage it was! Almost a record, I should think. We were thirty-two days getting to Southampton; but that was because we had halts on the way and were convoyed by some of the British warships which have worked such marvels in this war. We had with us a noble cruiser which on a later day, though we thought her slow, knocked more speed out of herself than the builders ever dreamed of, and that was when she helped to sink the German warships off the Falkland Islands.

By the time we reached the south of England some big things had happened, and we were keener than ever to get to the front. We had not long to wait. We landed, and in less than a week we left England and crossed over to

France, where we went into billets for four days, to settle down. From the billets we marched nearly seven miles and went into trenches. For three full months, in the worst time of a very bad year, I ate and drank, and slept and fought, in trenches, with intervals in billets, sometimes up to the hips in water and often enough sleeping on a thick couch of mud. I cannot go into too much detail, but I can say that our officers always tried to go one better than the Germans, for the sake of the men—and for the most part they succeeded. We have picked up a lot from the Germans in this trench game. They have a main trench and about four trenches behind that, the first of the four being about twenty yards away; so that if you knock them out of one you knock them into another.

That march to the trenches was a thing that can never be forgotten. It was very dark and raining heavily, so that we were thoroughly soaked; but we had no time to think of that, for we were bound for the firing line, we were going to fight for the first time, and we wondered who amongst us would be absent when the next roll was called. The trench to which we were bound was in its little way famous. It had been the scene of some terrible fighting. The Indian troops were holding it, but they had been driven out by the Germans, who took possession and thought they were going to hold it; but the Connaught Rangers made a desperate charge, routed the Germans with the bayonet and retook the trenches. The Connaughts won, but at a very heavy cost, and about 150 of the brave fellows fell and were buried near the little bit of sodden, muddy ground on which they had fought. It was to relieve the Connaughts that we went into the trenches on La Bassée Road that stormy night.

It was not a very cheerful beginning, and as much unlike going into action as anything you can imagine. But we felt queer, this being our first taste of fighting, as we slipped into the trenches with our rifles loaded and prepared to fire in the wild night at an enemy we could not see. As soon as we went into the trenches we were ankle-deep in mud, and we were in mud, day and night, for seventy-two hours without a break. That was the beginning of three solid months of a sort of animal life in trenches and dug-outs, with occasional breaks for the change and rest in billets without which it would not be possible to live.

In a storm-swept trench—a barricade trench we called it—pointing my rifle at an enemy I could not see, I fired my first shot in battle. My section of thirteen men was in the trench which was nearest to the Germans, and that meant that we were separated from them by only a very few dozen yards. An officer of the Connaughts had given a descriptive object to fire at, and this was a small white outhouse which could be dimly made out in the darkness. The outhouse had the German trenches just in front of it, and we made a target of the building in the hope of potting the men in the trenches.

The order came, one man up and one man down, which meant that a man who was firing was standing for two hours and the man who was down was sitting or otherwise resting, or observing, as we call it.

Throughout that long night we kept up fire from the trenches, all anxious for the day to break, so that we could see what sort of a place we were in and what we were doing; but when the melancholy morning broke there was nothing to see in front of us except the portholes of the German trenches.

We had got through the first night of battle safely and had given the Germans good-morning with what we came to call the "awaking fire," though it sent many a man to sleep for the last time—and we were settling down to make some tea. That was shortly after midday of our first day in the trenches. I was working "partners" with my left-hand man, Private Smith, who said, "I'll just have a look to see what's going on."

He popped his head over the top of the trench and almost instantly he fell into my arms, for he had been shot—there must have been a sniper waiting for him—and had received what proved to be a most extraordinary wound. A bullet had struck him on the side of the head, just below the ear, and gone clean through and out at the other side, leaving a hole on each side.

"I'm hit!" said Smith, as he fell—that was all.

I was badly upset, as this was the first man I had seen shot, and being my special chum it came home to me; but I didn't let that prevent me from doing my best for him. Smith was quite conscious, and a plucky chap, and he knew that there was nothing for it but to see it through till night came. We bandaged him up as best we could and he had to lie there, in the mud and water and misery, till it was dark, then he was able to walk away from the trench to the nearest first-aid station, where the doctor complimented him on his courage and told him what an extraordinary case it was and what a miraculous escape he had had. Later on Smith was invalided home.

During the whole of that first spell in trenches we had no water to drink except what we fetched from a natural trench half-a-mile away. Men volunteered for this duty, which was very dangerous, as it meant hurrying over open ground, and the man who was fetching the water was under fire all the time, both going and coming, if the Germans saw him. This job was usually carried out a little before daybreak, when there was just light enough for the man to see, and not enough for the Germans to spot him; and a chap was always thankful when he was safely back in the trench and under cover.

At the end of the seventy-two hours we left the trenches. We came out at ten o'clock at night, expecting to be out for three days. We marched to an old barn which had been pretty well blown to pieces by shells, and into it we went; but it was no better than the trenches. The rain poured on to us through the shattered roof and it was bitterly cold, so that I could not sleep. We had everything on, so as to be ready for a call instantly, and without so much as a blanket I was thoroughly miserable. Instead of having three days off we were ordered to go into a fresh lot of trenches, and next afternoon we marched into them and there we stayed for six weeks, coming out seven or eight times. In these trenches we were in dug-outs, so that we got a change from standing sometimes hip-deep in mud and water by getting into the dug-out and resting there. A dug-out was simply a hole made in the side of the trench, high enough to be fairly dry and comfortable.

During the whole of these six weeks it meant practically death to show yourself, and so merciless was the fire that for the whole of the time a dead German soldier was lying on the ground about a hundred yards away from us. He was there when we went and was still there when we left. We could not send out a party to bury him and the Germans themselves never troubled about the poor beggar. One day a chum of mine, named Tobin, was on the look-out when his rifle suddenly cracked, and he turned round and said, "I've hit one." And so he had, for he had knocked a German over not far away and no doubt killed him.

What with the weather and the mud and the constant firing we had a very bad time. Each night we had four hours' digging, which was excessively hard work, and if we were not digging we were fetching rations in for the company. These rations had to be fetched at night from carts three-quarters of a mile away, which was the nearest the drivers dare bring them. These expeditions were always interesting, because we never knew what we were going to get—sometimes it would be a fifty-pound tin of biscuits and sometimes a bag of letters or a lot of cigarettes, but whatever it was we took it to our dug-outs, just as animals take food to their holes, and the things were issued next morning.

One way and another we had between fifty and sixty men wounded in our own particular trenches, mostly by rifle fire, though occasionally a shell would burst near us and do a lot of mischief; and what was happening in our own trenches was taking place all around La Bassée. We should have suffered much more heavily if we had not been provided with periscopes, which have saved many a precious life and limb.

We paid very little attention to the German shell fire, and as for the "Jack Johnsons" we took them as much as a matter of course as we took our breakfast. Some of the German artillery fire actually amused us, and this was when they got their mortars to work. We could see the shot coming and often enough could dodge it, though frequently the great fat thing would drive into the ground and smother us with mud. For some of the German artillery fire we were really very thankful, because in their rage they were smashing up some farm buildings not far away from us. The cause of our gratitude was that this shelling saved us the trouble of cutting down and chopping firewood for warmth and cooking in the trenches. When night came we simply went to the farmhouse, and the firewood, in the shape of shattered doors and beams and furniture, was waiting for us. The farm people had left, so we were able to help ourselves to chickens, which we did, and a glorious change they were on the everlasting bully beef. A chicken doesn't go very far with hungry soldiers, and on one occasion we had a chicken apiece, and remarkably good they were too, roasted in the trenches. Another great time was when we caught a little pig at the farm and killed it and took it to the trenches, where we cooked it.

When we had finished with the second lot of trenches we went into a third set, and I was there till I was wounded and sent home. These trenches were only about a hundred and twenty yards from the second lot, so that the whole of the three months I spent in trenches was passed in a very little area of ground, an experience which is so totally different from that of so many of our soldiers who were out at the war at the very beginning, and covered such great distances in marching from place to place and battle to battle. These chaps were lucky, because they got the change of scene and the excitement of big fighting, but the only change we had was in going out of one trench into another.

It was now the middle of December and bitter weather, but we were cheered up by the thought of Christmas, and found that things were getting much more lively than they had been. One night a splendid act was performed by Lieutenant Seckham, one of our platoon officers, and two of our privates, Cunningham and Harris.

An officer of the Royal Engineers had gone out to fix up some barbed wire entanglements in front of our trenches. The Germans were firing heavily at the time, and they must have either seen or heard the officer at work. They went for him and struck him down and there he lay in the open. To leave the trenches was a most perilous thing to do, but Mr. Seckham and the two men got out and on to the open ground, and bit by bit they made their way to the Engineer officer, got hold of him, and under a furious fire brought him right along and into our trench, and we gave a cheer which rang out in the night above the firing and told the Germans that their frantic efforts had failed. Mr. Seckham was a splendid officer in every way and we were greatly grieved when, not long afterwards, he was killed. Another of our fine young platoon officers, Lieutenant Townsend, has been killed since I came home.

We were so near the Germans at times that we could throw things at them and they could hurl things at us, and we both did, the things being little bombs, after the style of the old hand-grenade. We got up a bomb-throwing class and hurled our bombs; but it was not possible to throw them very far—only twenty-five yards or so. The West Yorkshires, who were near us, got a great many of these missiles thrown at them, but they did not all explode. One day a sergeant of ours—Jarvis—was out getting wood when he saw one of them lying on the ground. He picked it up and looked at it, then threw it down and instantly it exploded, and he had no fewer than forty-three wounds, mostly cuts, caused by the flying fragments, so that the bomb made a proper mess of him.

"We were so near the Germans that they could hurl bombs at us."

Our own bombs were made of ordinary pound jam tins, filled with explosive and so on, like a little shell, which, as the case of the sergeant showed, was not anything like as sweet a thing to get as jam. The Germans were very fond of flinging these hand-bombs and seemed to have a great idea of their value in attacks and defence.

Christmas Eve was with us, Christmas Day was soon to dawn—and what a strange and terrible Christmas it was to be!

On Christmas Eve itself we plainly heard the Germans shouting.

"A merry Christmas to you!" they said, and there was no mistaking the German voices that came to us in our trenches out of the darkness.

"A merry Christmas to you!"

Again the Germans greeted us, though we could not see them, and there was something pathetic in the words, which were shouted in a lull in the fighting. Some of our men answered the wish, but I did not—I had no heart to do so, when I knew that the message meant so little.

It may have been a matter of sentiment, because this was the time of peace on earth and goodwill towards men, or it may not; but at any rate the order came that if the Germans did not fire we were not to fire. But Christmas or no Christmas, and in spite of their greetings, the Germans went on firing, and we were forced to do the same, so throughout the night of Christmas Eve we had our rifles going and did not stop till it was daylight.

But the rifle fire was not the only sound of warfare that was heard—there was the sharp booming of artillery. The field batteries were hard at it and we knew they must be doing fearful mischief amongst the Germans. The night became truly awful; but how dreadful we did not know till Christmas Day itself, then, the firing having ceased, we saw that the ground in front of us, not very far away, was littered with the German dead.

A Merry Christmas!

The very men who had sent the greeting to us were lying dead within our sight, for the Germans had started to change their position and the British shells had shattered them. Something like two hundred and fifty of the Germans were lying dead upon the field, and sorry indeed must the dawn of Christmas Day have been to those who were left.

Peace on earth! There *was* peace of a sort, for as we looked on the German dead from our trenches we saw two Germans appear in full view, holding up their hands, to show us that they were unarmed.

You can imagine what a solemn spectacle that was—what a Christmas Day it was which dawned upon us in the trenches. We knew instinctively what was wanted—the ground was littered with the German dead and the Germans wanted an armistice so that they could bury them.

One of our officers went out and talked with the two Germans who were holding up their hands—covered by British rifles. He soon learned what they wanted, and the armistice was granted.

It was about three o'clock in the afternoon of Christmas Day when the Germans set to work to bury their dead, and as they did so we left our trenches and stood on the open ground and watched them. We saw them perfectly clearly, because the main German trench was not more than 120 yards away, and the burial took place a few yards behind this.

I have seen a photograph of British and German soldiers fraternising on Christmas Day; but there was nothing of this sort with us. The only incident I witnessed was a British officer shaking hands with a German officer. That was all. I did not shake hands with them—and I had not the least wish to do so, though I bore them no ill-will on that sad Christmas Day.

I was thankful when Christmas was over and we had settled down to ordinary routine work, killing and being killed, for it is astonishing how soon you get accustomed to the business of firing on and being fired at.

The trenches had got from bad to worse. When I first went into them there was eighteen inches of water and five inches of mud; but now it was a matter of standing almost up to the waist in water. They became so bad that instead of using the communication trenches, which you might almost call tunnels, it was decided that we should cross the open country to get to our fighting-place, the main trench—indeed, we had no option, because the communication trench was almost impassable.

On a mid-January night, and very bad at that, we began the journey to the trenches. If there had been just ordinary honest darkness we should have been all right and quite satisfied; but though there was darkness enough there was plenty of light—the uncanny brightness which came from the star-shells.

Star-shells were going up all along the line and bursting. They are a sort of firework, giving a brilliant light, and as they exploded they showed us up almost as clearly as if we had been in daylight.

We had only a very short distance to go, but the star-lights made the journey to the trenches a desperate undertaking.

In single file, a little bunch of ten of us, crouching down, holding our loaded rifles and carrying all we possessed—we went along, losing no time.

From the stealthy way in which we started on our little trip you might have thought that we were burglars or villains bent on some fearsome job, instead of ordinary British soldiers getting back to their trenches.

We went with caution, and had not covered more than ten yards when what I take to be machine-gun fire was opened on us.

All at once, without the slightest warning, a real hail of bullets struck us, and of the ten men of us who were advancing in single file three were killed and four were wounded. The three who were shot down in the ghastly glare of the star-shells were ahead of me.

When that happened we were ordered to keep well apart and open out, but there was not much chance for those of us who were left; at any rate, no sooner had we obeyed and were making a little headway than I was struck myself on the head.

For half-an-hour or so I was unconscious; then I recovered and picked myself up and found that I was all alone. I crawled a few yards to a trench and got into it; but finding it full of water I thought I might as well be killed as drowned, so I got out, and not caring in the least for the German bullets or the star-shells, I made my way as best I could to the nearest dressing-station, and received attention. After that I found myself in a motor-car, and later at a clearing-station and on the boat for home.

You can see the scar of the wound here; but I don't bother about that. I suffer terribly from sleeplessness—and too often I see again the German soldiers who had wished us a merry Christmas—and were buried at the back of their trenches on the gloomy afternoon of Christmas Day.

British and German descendants of World War I veterans shake hands in commemoration of the Christmas 1914 truce - Image: Alan Cleaver

Chapter IX – Sapping and Mining: The "Lucky Company"

Sapper William Bell, Royal Engineers.

[In blowing up bridges, repairing the ravages of the enemy, in throwing pontoons over rivers, and in countless other ways, the Royal Engineers have contributed largely to the success of the British operations in the war. These splendid men, known a century ago as the Royal Sappers and Miners, have not only worked with the greatest energy since the war began, but they have also seen some hard fighting. This story of Sapper William Bell, 23rd Field Company, Royal Engineers, gives a picture of the many-sided operations of the magnificent corps whose mottoes are "Everywhere" and "Where right and glory lead."\]

SHEER hard work was the order of the day for our chaps from the time I landed in France from an old Irish cattle-boat till the day when I was packed off back to England suffering from rheumatic fever.

We worked excessively hard, and so did everybody else. Wherever there was an obstacle it had to go, and the infantry themselves time after time slaved away at digging and clearing, all of which was over and above the strain of the fighting and tremendous marching. It was a rare sight to see the Guards sweeping down the corn with their bayonets—sickles that reaped many a grim harvest then and later.

It was during the early stage of the war that bridges were blown up in wholesale fashion to check the German advance, and the work being particularly dangerous we had some very narrow escapes. A very near thing happened at Soissons.

We had been ordered to blow up a bridge, and during the day we charged it with gun-cotton, and were waiting to set the fuse until the last of our troops had crossed over. That was a long business, and exciting enough for anybody, because for hours the men of a whole division were passing, and all the time that great passing body of men, horses, guns, waggons and so on, was under a heavy artillery fire from the Germans.

At last the bridge was clear—it had served its purpose; the division was on the other side of the river, and all that remained to be done was to blow up the bridge. Three sections of our company retired, and the remaining section was left behind to attend to the fuse.

Very soon we heard a terrific report, and the same awful thought occurred to many of us—that there had been a premature explosion and that the section was lost. One of my chums, judging by the time of the fuse, said it was certain that the section was blown up, and indeed it was actually reported that an officer and a dozen men had been killed.

But, to our intense relief, we learned that the report was wrong; but we heard also how narrowly our fellows had escaped, and how much they owed to the presence of mind and coolness of the officer. It seems that as soon as the fuse was fired the lieutenant instinctively suspected that something was wrong, and instantly ordered the men to lie flat, with the result that they were uninjured by the tremendous upheaval of masonry, though they were a bit shaken when they caught us up on the road later. This incident gives a good idea of the sort of work and the danger that the Royal Engineers were constantly experiencing in the earlier stages of the war, so that one can easily understand what is happening now in the bitter winter-time.

An Engineer, like the referee in a football match, sees a lot of the game, and it was near a French village that we had a fine view of a famous affair.

We had been sent to the spot on special duty, and were resting on the crest of a hill, watching the effects of the enemy's field-guns.

Suddenly in the distance we saw figures moving. At first we could not clearly make them out, but presently we saw that they were Algerian troops, and that there seemed to be hosts of them. They swarmed on swiftly, and took up a position in some trenches near us.

The Algerians, like our Indian troops, hate trench fighting, and long to come to grips with the enemy. We knew this well enough, but we realised the peril of leaving cover and advancing towards an enemy who was very close, and who was sweeping the ground with an uncommonly deadly fire.

Putting all fear aside, remembering only their intense desire to come to grips, giving no thought to what must happen to them, the Algerians with enthusiastic shouts sprang from the trenches and bounded, like the sons of the desert they are, across the shell-swept zone that separated them from the annihilating gunfire of the enemy.

What happened was truly terrible. The Algerians were literally mowed down, as they charged across the deadly zone, and for a piece of sheer recklessness I consider that this attack was as good—or as bad—as the charge of the Light Brigade.

The Algerians were cut to pieces in the mad attempt to reach the German batteries, and the handful of survivors were forced to retire. To their everlasting credit be it said that, in withdrawing under that terrible fire, they did their best to bring their wounded men away. They picked up as many of the fallen as they could and slung them across the shoulder, as the best way of carrying them out of danger.

I shall never forget the scene that met my eyes when we returned to the village. Women were weeping and wringing their hands as the survivors carried their wounded through the streets—for the French are deeply attached to their Colonial troops—and the men of the place were nearly as bad; even some of our chaps, who are not too easily moved, were upset.

While in this locality we had a very warm time of it, for we were continuously under artillery fire. We were in a remarkably good position for seeing the battle, some of our batteries being on our right, some on our left, and the German guns in front. It was really hot work, and when we were not hard at it carrying out our own duties, we took cover on the other side of a hill near the road; but some of our men got rather tired of cover, and found the position irksome; but if you so much as showed yourself you were practically done for. One day our trumpeter exposed himself, just for a moment; but it was enough. He was instantly struck and badly wounded.

At another time we were in our sleeping-quarters in a school-house, and had an escape that was truly miraculous. We had settled down and were feeling pretty comfortable, when the Germans suddenly started shelling us; suddenly, too, with a terrific crash, a shell dropped and burst in the very midst of us.

Theoretically, the lot of us in that school-house ought to have been wiped out by this particular shell, but the extraordinary fact is that though every one was badly shaken up, only one of our men was wounded—all the rest of us escaped. Luckily we had the hospital men at hand, and the poor chap who had been knocked over was taken away at once to the doctors.

We had had a very hard, hot time, and were glad when the French came and relieved us, and gave our division a bit of rest and change. The Germans in that particular part were thoroughly beaten, and a batch of 500 who were covering the retreat were captured by the French.

They had started for Paris, and were very near it when they were bagged. I dare say they got to Paris all right. So did we, for we entrained for the city, but stayed there less than an hour. I had a chance of seeing something of the thorough way in which Paris had been prepared for defence, and on my way to Ypres I noticed how extensively the bridges that were likely to be of any use to the Germans had been destroyed. The loss in bridges alone in this great war has been stupendous.

When we entered Ypres it was a beautiful old cathedral city; now it is a shapeless mass of ruins, a melancholy centre of the longest and deadliest battle that has ever been fought in the history of the world. We had a rousing reception from the British troops who were already in the city, and a specially warm greeting from our own R.E. men, who gave me a huge quantity of pipes, tobacco and cigarettes from home, to divide amongst our company.

"We had a very warm time of it."

We were soon in the thick of the fiercest and most eventful part of the fighting. We were put to work digging trenches for the infantry and fixing up wire entanglements. The wire was in coils half a mile long, and what with that and the barbs and the weight, the carrying and dragging and fixing was a truly fearsome job.

And not only that, but it was extremely dangerous, because we were constantly under fire—sometimes we were fixing up wire within a few hundred yards of the German lines. Before getting to Ypres we had covering parties of infantry to protect us from snipers and sudden attacks; but at Ypres this protection was rarely given, because of the very heavy pressure on the firing line. We were ceaselessly sniped; but on the whole our casualties were remarkably few—but we were always known as the "Lucky Company."

In addition to doing this hard and dangerous work, we were roughing it with a vengeance. Our sleeping-quarters were dug-outs in a wood, and were lined with straw, when we could get it. The enemy always make a special point of "searching" woods with shells, and we were so situated that we were pestered day and night by the German gunners, who were hoping to draw our artillery fire and so locate our own batteries. Anything like rest was utterly out of the question owing to these artillery duels, which were the bane of our life.

Silence was essential for our work, and we used muffled mauls—our big wooden mallets.

One moonlight night we were going to our usual duties when a shell flew past, exploding with terrific force within ten paces of us. We took it to be one of the Germans' random shots, but after going a short distance we had more shells bursting about us, and bullets whizzing, telling us that the enemy's snipers were at it again. Once more we justified our nickname of the "Lucky Company," for we had only one man hit—a fine chap, whose fighting qualities were well known to us, so we grinned when he said to me, after being struck on the shoulder, "I should like to have a look at that German, Bill!"

In the moonlight we offered a first-rate target to the hidden German snipers, and they certainly ought to have done more with us than just hit one man; but compared with British soldiers, the Germans, with rare exceptions, are only "third-class" shots. I have mentioned this little affair chiefly by way of showing the constant danger to which field engineers are exposed.

The Germans at that time had their eyes on us properly, and the very next day they did their level best to make up for their sorry performance in the moonlight.

We had been told off to dig trenches for the infantry on our left, and we started out on the job. Rain had been falling heavily, the ground was like a quagmire, and we had to struggle through marshy ground and ploughed fields.

This was bad enough in all conscience, but to help to fill the cup of our misery the German snipers got at us, and gave us what was really a constant hail of bullets. We floundered on, doing our dead best to reach a certain wood. After floundering for some time, we were ordered to halt. By that time we had reached the wood, and the fire was truly awful.

Behind our tool-carts we usually fasten a big biscuit-tin, which is a big metal case, and as the sniping became particularly furious, four of our men bolted for shelter behind the biscuit-tin. I don't know what it is in the British soldier that makes him see the humour of even a fatal situation, but it happened that the rest of us were so tickled at the sight of our comrades scuttling that we burst out laughing.

But we didn't laugh long, for shells as well as bullets came, and we saw that the Germans were concentrating their fire upon us. They were going for all they were worth at the wood, and our only chance of safety lay in securing cover. We made a dash for the trees, and I sheltered behind one.

Then an extraordinary thing happened. A shell came and literally chopped down the tree. The shell spared my life, but the tumbling tree nearly got me. Luckily I skipped aside, and just escaped from being crushed to death by the crashing timber.

The firing was kept up for a long time after that, but we went on with our work and finished it, and then we were ordered to occupy the trenches we had just dug. We were glad to get into them, and it was pleasant music to listen to our own infantry, who had come into action, and were settling the accounts of some of the German snipers.

Later on we were told to get to a farmhouse, and we did, and held it for some hours, suffering greatly from thirst and hunger, in consequence of having missed our meals since the early morning. Some of our tool-carts had been taken back by the infantry, and this was a far more perilous task than some people might think, for the carts are usually filled with detonators, containing high explosives like gun-cotton, and an exploding shell hitting a cart would cause devastation.

The farmhouse was ranked as a "safe place," and we reckoned that we were lucky to get inside it; but it proved anything but lucky, and I grieve to say that it was here that my particular chum, an old schoolmate, met his death. We had scarcely reached the "safe place" when the cursed shells began to burst again, and I said to myself that we were bound to get some souvenirs. And we did.

My comrades had brought their tea to a hut, and I went there to get my canteen to take to the cookhouse. No sooner had I left the hut than I heard a fearful explosion. One gets used to these awful noises, and I took no notice of it at the time; but shortly afterwards I was told that my chum had been hit, and I rushed back to the hut. Terrible was the sight that met me. Eight of our men were lying wounded, amongst them my friend. With a heavy heart I picked him up, and he died in my arms soon afterwards. Two other men died before their injuries could be attended to—and this single shell also killed two officers' chargers.

It was soon after this that I went through what was perhaps my most thrilling experience. Again it was night, and we were engaged in our usual work, when suddenly we heard the sound of heavy rifle fire. Throwing down our tools, we grabbed our rifles. We had not the slightest idea of what was happening, but looking cautiously over the parapet of the trench which we were working on, we could dimly see dark figures in front, and took them to be Germans.

We were ordered to fire, the word being passed from man to man to take careful aim; but owing to the darkness this was not an easy thing to do. We fired, and instantly we were greeted with terrific shouting, and we knew that the Germans were charging. Not an instant was lost. With fixed bayonets, out from the trench we jumped, the infantry on our right and left doing the same.

Carrying out a bayonet charge is an experience I shall never forget. One loses all sense of fear, and thinks of nothing but going for and settling the enemy. For my own part I distinctly recollect plunging my bayonet into a big, heavy German, and almost instantly afterwards clubbing another with the butt of my rifle. It was only a short fight, but a very fierce one. The Germans gave way, leaving their dead and wounded behind them.

When the charge was over we went back to our trenches, taking our wounded with us. Our company's casualties numbered about a dozen, the majority of the men suffering from more or less serious wounds; but we were pretty well satisfied, and felt that we had earned our sleep that night.

The next day I had another close shave, a shell bursting very near me and killing twelve horses belonging to the 15th Hussars, who were on patrol duty.

After seven weeks of this famous and awful fighting at Ypres, I was taken ill with rheumatic fever—and no wonder, after such work, and sleeping in such places as we were forced to occupy. After a spell in the hospital at Ypres, I was moved on from place to place, till I made the final stage of the journey to England.

A remarkable thing happened during one of the heavy bombardments that we endured. A shell came and fell plump in the midst of us, and it really seemed as if we were all doomed. But the shell did not explode, and on examining the cap, it was found to bear the number "23." That, you will remember, is the number of my own company, so you can understand that we felt more justified than ever in calling ourselves the "Lucky Company."

Chapter X - L Battery's Heroic Last Stand

Gunner H. Derbyshire, Royal Horse Artillery.

[Not one of the almost numberless valiant deeds of the war has proved more thrilling and splendid than the exploit of L Battery, Royal Horse Artillery, at Nery, near Compiègne, on September 1st, 1914. After greatly distinguishing itself at Mons, the battery helped to cover the retreat of the Allies, and fought a heavy rearguard action. On the last day of the retirement the battery unexpectedly came into action at very close range with an overwhelmingly superior German force. So destructive was the fire which was brought to bear on the battery that only one British gun was left in action, and this was served, until all the ammunition was expended, by Battery-Sergeant-Major Dorrell, Sergeant Nelson, Gunner H. Darbyshire and Driver Osborne, all the rest of the officers and men of the battery having been killed or wounded. At the close of the artillery duel the Queen's Bays and I Battery came to the rescue, and the shattered remnant of L Battery came triumphant out of the tremendous fray. This story is told by Gunner Darbyshire, who, with Driver Osborne, was awarded the great distinction of the Médaille Militaire of France, while the sergeant-major and Sergeant Nelson for their gallantry were promoted to second-lieutenants, and awarded the Victoria Cross.]

As soon as we got into touch with the Germans—and that was at Mons—they never left us alone. We had a hot time with them, but we gave them a hotter. Mons was a terrible experience, especially to men going straight into action for the first time, and so furious was the artillery duel that at its height some of the British and German shells actually struck each other in the air. In less than an hour we fired nearly six hundred rounds—the full number carried by a battery of six guns. But I must not talk of Mons; I will get to the neighbourhood of Compiègne, and tell of the fight that was sprung on the battery and left only three survivors.

All through the retreat we had been fighting heavily, and throughout the day on August 31st we fought till four o'clock in the afternoon; then we were ordered to retire to Compiègne. It was a long march, and when we got to Nery, near Compiègne, early in the evening, both horses and men were utterly exhausted and very hungry. As soon as we got in we gave the horses some food—with the mounted man the horse always comes first—and made ourselves as comfortable as possible.

Outposts were put out by the officers, and the cavalry who were with us, the 2nd Dragoon Guards (Queen's Bays), were in a small field on the side of a road which was opposite to us. That road was really a deep cutting, and I want you to bear it in mind, because it largely proved the salvation of the few survivors of the battery at the end of the fight. For the rest, the country was just of the sort you can see in many places in England—peaceful, fertile and prosperous, with farms dotted about, but nobody left on them, for the warning had been given that the German hordes were marching, and the people had fled in terror.

Having made all our dispositions, we went to sleep, and rested till half-past three in the morning, when we were roused and told to get ready to march at a moment's notice.

The darkness seemed to hang about more than usual, and the morning was very misty; but we did not pay much attention to that, and we breakfasted and fed the horses. We expected to be off again, but the battery was ordered to stand fast until further notice.

In war-time never a moment is wasted, and Sergeant-Major Dorrell thought that this would be a good opportunity to water the horses, so he ordered the right half-battery to water, and the horses were taken behind a sugar factory which was a little distance away. The horses were watered and brought back and hooked into the guns and waggons; then the left half-battery went to water.

Everything was perfectly quiet. Day had broken, and the landscape was hidden in the grey veil of the early morning. All was well, it seemed, and we were now expecting to move off. A ridge about 600 yards away was, we supposed, occupied by French cavalry, and a general and orderly retreat was going on in our rear. Then, without the slightest warning, a "ranging" shot was dropped into the battery, and we knew instantly that the Germans were on us and had fired this trial shot to get the range of us.

Immediately after this round was fired the whole place was alive with shrapnel and maxim bullets, and it was clear that the battery was almost surrounded by German artillery and infantry. As a matter of fact, the French cavalry had left their position on the ridge before daybreak, and a strong German force, with ten guns and two maxims, had advanced under cover of the mist and occupied the position, which was an uncommonly good one for artillery.

We were taken completely by surprise, and at first could do nothing, for the "ranging" shot was followed by an absolute hail of shrapnel, which almost blew the battery to pieces.

The very beginning of the German fire made havoc amongst the battery and the Bays, and the losses amongst the horses were particularly severe and crippling. But we soon pulled ourselves together, with a fierce determination to save the battery, and to do our best to give the Germans a vast deal more than they were giving us.

"Who'll volunteer to get the guns into action?" shouted Captain Bradbury.

Every man who could stand and fight said "Me!" and there was an instant rush for the guns. Owing to heavy losses in our battery, I had become limber gunner, and it was part of my special duty to see to the ammunition in the limbers. But special duties at a time like that don't count for much; the chief thing is to keep the guns going, and it was now a case of every one, officer and man, striving his best to save the battery. The officers, while they lived and could keep up at all, were noble, and worked exactly like the men. From start to finish of that fatal fight they set a glorious example.

We rushed to the guns, I say, and with the horses, when they were living and unhurt, and man-handling when the poor beasts were killed or maimed, we made shift to bring as heavy a fire as we could raise against the Germans. The advantage was clearly and undoubtedly with them—they were in position, they had our range, and they had far more guns and men, while we had half our horses watering by the sugar mill and shells were thick in the air and ploughing up the earth before we could get a single gun into action.

Let me stop for a minute to explain what actually happened to the guns, so that you can understand the odds against us as we fought. The guns, as you have seen, were ready for marching, not for fighting, which we were not expecting; half the horses were away, many at the guns were killed or wounded, and officers and men had suffered fearfully in the course literally of a few seconds after the "ranging" shot plumped into us.

The first gun came to grief through the terrified horses bolting and overturning it on the steep bank of the road in front of us; the second gun had the spokes of a wheel blown out by one of the very first of the German shells, the third was disabled by a direct hit with a shell which killed the detachment; the fourth was left standing, though the wheels got knocked about and several holes were made in the limber, and all the horses were shot down. The fifth gun was brought into action, but was silenced by the detachment being killed, and the sixth gun, our own, remained the whole time, though the side of the limber was blown away, the wheels were severely damaged, holes were blown in the shield, and the buffer was badly peppered by shrapnel bullets. The gun was a wreck, but, like many another wreck, it held gallantly on until the storm was over—and it was saved at last.

In a shell fire that was incessant and terrific, accompanied by the hail of bullets from the maxims, we got to work.

We had had some truly tremendous cannonading at Mons; but this was infinitely worse, for the very life of the battery was in peril, and it was a point-blank battle, just rapid, ding-dong kill-fire, our own shells and the Germans' bursting in a fraction of time after leaving the muzzles of the guns.

As soon as we were fairly in action, the Germans gave us a fiercer fire than ever, and it is only just to them to say that their practice was magnificent; but I think we got the pull of them, crippled and shattered though we were—nay, I know we did, for when the bloody business was all over, we counted far more of the German dead than all our battery had numbered at the start.

The thirteen-pounders of the Royal Horse Artillery can be fired at the rate of fifteen rounds a minute, and though we were not perhaps doing that, because we were short-handed and the limbers were about thirty yards away, still we were making splendid practice, and it was telling heavily on the Germans.

As the mist melted away we could at that short distance see them plainly—and they made a target which we took care not to miss. We went for the German guns and fighting men, and the Germans did all they knew to smash us—but they didn't know enough, and failed.

As soon as we got number six gun into action I jumped into the seat and began firing, but so awful was the concussion of our own explosions and the bursting German shells that I could not bear it for long. I kept it up for about twenty minutes, then my nose and ears were bleeding because of the concussion, and I could not fire anymore, so I left the seat and got a change by fetching ammunition.

And now there happened one of those things which, though they seem marvellous, are always taking place in time of war, and especially such a war as this, when life is lost at every turn. Immediately after I left the seat, Lieutenant Campbell, who had been helping with the ammunition, took it, and kept the firing up without the loss of a second of time; but he had not fired more than a couple of rounds when a shell burst under the shield. The explosion was awful, and the brave young officer was hurled about six yards away from the very seat in which I had been sitting a few seconds earlier. There is no human hope against such injuries, and Mr. Campbell lived for only a few minutes.

Another officer who fell quickly while doing dangerous work was Lieutenant Mundy, my section officer. He was finding the range and reporting the effects of our shells. To do that he had left the protection of the shield and was sitting on the ground alongside the gun wheel. This was a perilous position, being completely exposed to the shells which were bursting all around. Mr. Mundy was killed by an exploding shell which also wounded me. A piece of the shell caught me just behind the shoulder-blade. I felt it go into my back, but did not take much notice of it at the time, and went on serving the gun. Mr. Mundy had taken the place of Mr. Marsden, the left-section officer. The latter had gone out from home with us; but he had been badly wounded at Mons, where a shrapnel bullet went through the roof of his mouth and came out of his neck. In spite of that dreadful injury, however, he stuck bravely to his section.

I am getting on a bit too fast, perhaps, so I will return to the time when I had to leave the seat of the gun owing to the way in which the concussion had affected me. When I felt a little better I began to help Driver Osborne to fetch ammunition from the waggons. I had just managed to get back to the gun with an armful of ammunition, when a lyddite shell exploded behind me, threw me to the ground, and partly stunned me.

I was on the ground for what seemed to be about five minutes and thought I was gone; but when I came round I got up and found that I was uninjured. On looking round, however, I saw that Captain Bradbury, who had played a splendid part in getting the guns into action, had been knocked down by the same shell that floored me. I had been thrown on my face, Captain Bradbury had been knocked down backwards, and he was about two yards away from me. When I came to my senses I went up to him and saw that he was mortally wounded. He expired a few minutes afterwards. Though the captain knew that death was very near, he thought of his men to the last, and repeatedly begged to be carried away, so that they should not be upset by seeing him or hearing the cries which he could not restrain. Two of the men who were wounded, and were lying in the shelter of a neighbouring haystack, crawled up and managed to take the captain back with them; but he died almost as soon as the haystack was reached.

By this time our little camp was an utter wreck. Horses and men were lying everywhere, some of the horses absolutely blown to pieces; waggons and guns were turned upside down, and all around was the ruin caused by the German shells. The camp was littered with fragments of shell and our own cartridge-cases, while the ground looked as if it had been ploughed and harrowed anyhow. Nearly all the officers and men had been either killed or wounded.

It is no exaggeration to say that the Germans literally rained shrapnel and bullets on us. A German shell is filled with about three hundred bullets, so that with two or three shells bursting you get as big a cloud of bullets as you would receive from a battalion of infantry.

The Germans had ten of their guns and two machine-guns going, and it is simply marvellous that every man and horse in our battery was not destroyed. Bear in mind, too, that the German artillery was not all field-guns—they had big guns with them, and they fired into us with the simple object of wiping us out. That is quite all right, of course; but they never gave a thought to our wounded—they went for them just as mercilessly as they bombarded the rest.

There was a little farmhouse in our camp, an ordinary French farm building with a few round haystacks near it. When the fight began, we thought of using this building as a hospital; but it was so clear that the place was an absolute death-trap that we gave up that idea very quickly, and got our wounded under the shelter of one of the haystacks, where they were pretty safe so long as the stack did not catch fire, because a good thick stack will resist even direct artillery fire in a wonderful manner. But the Germans got their guns on this particular stack, and it was a very bad look-out for our poor, helpless fellows, many of whom had been badly mangled.

As for the farmhouse it was blown to pieces, as I saw afterwards when I visited it, and not a soul could have lived in the place. Walls, windows, roof, ceilings—all were smashed, and the furniture was in fragments. A building like that was a fair target; but the haystack was different, and the Germans did a thing that no British gunners would have done. At that short distance they could see perfectly clearly what was happening—they could see that as our wounded fell we got hold of them and dragged them out of the deadly hail to the shelter of the stack, about a score of yards away, to comparative safety. Noticing this, one of the German officers immediately concentrated a heavy shell fire on the heap of wounded—thirty or forty helpless men—in an attempt to set fire to the stack. That was a deliberate effort to destroy wounded men. We saw that, and the sight helped us to put more strength into our determination to smash the German guns.

The Germans were mad to wipe us out, and I know that for my own part I would not have fallen into their clutches alive. My mind was quite made up on that point, for I had seen many a British soldier who had fallen on the roadside, dead beat, and gone to sleep—and slept for the last time when the Germans came up. On a previous occasion we passed through one place where there had been a fight—it must have been in the darkness—and the wounded had been put in a cemetery, the idea being that the Germans would not touch a cemetery. That idea proved to be wrong. One of the German aeroplanes that were constantly hovering over the battery had given some German batteries our position, but we got away, and the German gunners, enraged at our escape, instantly dropped shells into the cemetery, to wipe the wounded out. If they would do that they would not hesitate to fire deliberately on our wounded under the haystack—and they did not hesitate.

It was not many minutes after the fight began in the mist when only number six gun was left in the battery, and four of us survived to serve it—the sergeant-major, who had taken command; Sergeant Nelson, myself, and Driver Osborne, and we fired as fast as we could in a noise that was now more terrible than ever and in a little camp that was utter wreckage. There was the ceaseless din of screaming, bursting shells, the cries of the wounded, for whom we could do something, but not much, and the cries of the poor horses, for which we could do nothing. The noise they made was like the grizzling of a child that is not well—a very pitiful sound, but, of course, on a much bigger scale; and that sound of suffering went up from everywhere around us, because everywhere there were wounded horses.

It was not long before we managed to silence several German guns. But very soon Sergeant Nelson was severely wounded by a bursting shell, and that left only three of us.

The Bays' horses, like our own, had been either killed or wounded or had bolted, but the men had managed to get down on the right of us and take cover under the steep bank of the road, and from that position, which was really a natural trench, they fired destructively on the Germans.

British cavalry, dismounted, have done some glorious work in this great war, but they have done nothing finer, I think, than their work near Compiègne on that September morning. And of all the splendid work there was none more splendid than the performance of a lance-corporal, who actually planted a maxim on his own knees and rattled into the Germans with it. There was plenty of kick in the job, but he held on gamely, and he must have done heavy execution with his six hundred bullets a minute.

This rifle and maxim fire of the Bays had a wonderful effect in silencing the German fire, and it helped us greatly when we came to the last stage of the duel.

I don't know how many of the Bays there were, but it was impossible for them to charge, even if they had had their horses, owing to the fact that the road in front of us was a deep cutting. If the cutting had not been there the Uhlans, who alone considerably outnumbered us, would have swept down on us and there would not have been anyone left in L Battery at any rate.

"He planted a maxim on his own knees and rattled into the Germans."

By the time we had practically silenced the German guns the three of us who were surviving were utterly exhausted. Osborne, who was kneeling beside a waggon wheel, had a narrow escape from being killed. A shell burst between the wheel and the waggon body, tore the wheel off, and sent the spokes flying all over the place. One of the spokes caught Osborne just over the ribs and knocked him over, backwards.

I looked round on hearing the explosion of the shell, and said, "I think Osborne's gone this time," but we were thankful to find that he was only knocked over. One of his ribs was fractured, but we did not know of this till afterwards.

Meanwhile, the men who had gone to water the horses of the left-half battery had heard the firing, and had tried hard to get back to help us; but they were met on the road by an officer, who said that the battery was practically annihilated, and it would be useless for them to return. The Germans had seen them watering the horses, and had begun to shell the sugar factory. This caused the remaining horses of the battery to gallop away, and a lot of them were killed as they galloped, though a good many got away and were afterwards found in the neighbouring town of Compiègne, wandering about. As for the men, they "mooched" in any direction as stragglers, and eventually we came up with them.

The three of us had served the gun and kept it in action till it was almost too hot to work, and we were nearly worn out; but we went on firing, and with a good heart, for we knew that the Germans had been badly pounded, that the Bays had them in a grip, and that another battery of horse-gunners was dashing to the rescue. On they came, in glorious style—there is no finer sight than that of a horse battery galloping into action.

Two or three miles away from us I Battery had heard the heavy firing, and knew that something must be happening to us. Round they turned, and on they dashed, taking everything before them and stopping for nothing till they reached a ridge about 2000 yards away; then they unlimbered and got into action, and never was there grander music heard than that which greeted the three of us who were left in L Battery when the saving shells of "I" screamed over us and put the finish to the German rout.

In a speech made to I Battery Sir John French said—

"No branch of the Service has done better work in this campaign than the Royal Horse Artillery. It is impossible to pick out one occasion more than another during this campaign on which I Battery has specially distinguished itself, because the battery has always done brilliant work. Your general tells me that you were in action continuously for ten days...."

We had been pretty well hammered out of existence, but we had a kick left in us, and we gave it, and what with this and the Bays and the bashing by the fresh battery, the Germans soon had enough of it, and for the time being they made no further effort to molest us.

At last the fight was finished. We had—thank God!—saved the guns, and the Germans, despite their frantic efforts, had made no progress, and had only a heap of dead and wounded and a lot of battered guns to show for their attempt to smash us in the morning mist. We had kept them off day after day, and we kept them off again. We had been badly punished, but we had mauled them terribly in the fight, which lasted about an hour.

Three of our guns had been disabled, two waggons blown up, and many wheels blown off the waggons.

Some strange things had happened between Mons and Compiègne, and now that the duel had ended we had a chance of recollecting them and counting up the cost to us. Corporal Wheeler Carnham was knocked down while trying to stop a runaway ammunition waggon, and one of the wheels went over his legs. He managed to get on his feet again, but he had no sooner done so than he was struck on the legs by a piece of shell. At Compiègne two gunners were blown to pieces and could not be identified. Driver Laws had both legs broken by a waggon which turned over at Mons, and afterwards the waggon was blown up, and he went with it. Shoeing-Smith Heath was standing alongside me at Compiègne when the firing began. I told him to keep his head down, but he didn't do so—and lost it. The farrier was badly wounded, and the quartermaster-sergeant was knocked down and run over by an ammunition waggon. Gunner Huddle, a signaller, was looking through his glasses to try to find out where the shells were coming from, when he was struck on the head by a piece of bursting shell.

Our commanding officer, Major the Hon. W. D. Sclater-Booth, was standing behind the battery, dismounted, as we all were, observing the fall of the shells, when he was hit by a splinter from a bursting shell and severely wounded. He was removed, and we did not see him again until we were on the way to the base. As far as I remember, he was taken off by one of the cavalry officers from the Bays.

Lieutenant Giffard, our right section officer, was injured early in the fight by a shell which shattered his left knee, and he was taken and placed with the rest of the wounded behind the haystack, where in a very short time they were literally piled up. As soon as the officers and men fell we did the best we could for them; but all we could do was just simply to drag them out of the danger of the bursting shells. Luckily, this particular haystack escaped fairly well, but very soon after the fight began nearly every haystack in the camp was blazing fiercely, set on fire by the German shells.

The first thing to be done after the fight was to bury our dead and collect our wounded, and in this sorrowful task we were helped by the Middlesex Regiment—the old "Die-Hards"—who have done so splendidly and suffered so heavily in this war. They, like I Battery, had come up, and we were very glad to see them. Some of our gallant wounded were beyond help, because of the shrapnel fire.

We buried our dead on the field where they had fallen, amidst the ruins of the battery they had fought to save, and with the fire and smoke still rising from the ruined buildings and the burning haystacks.

Another thing we did was to go round and shoot the poor horses that were hopelessly hurt—and a sorry task it was. One waggon we went to had five horses killed—only one horse was left out of the six which had been hooked in to march away in the mist of the morning; so we shot him and put him out of his misery. We had to shoot about twenty horses; but the rest were already dead, mostly blown to pieces and scattered over the field—a dreadful sight.

When we had buried the dead, collected our wounded, and destroyed our helpless horses, the guns of our battery were limbered up on to sound waggon limbers, and a pair of horses were borrowed from each sub-section of I Battery to take them away. Everything else was left behind—waggons, accoutrements, clothing, caps, and so on, and the battery was taken to a little village about four miles from Compiègne, where we tried to snatch a bit of rest; but we had no chance of getting it, owing to the harassing pursuit of big bodies of Uhlans.

From that time, until we reached the base, we wandered about as best we could, and managed to live on what we could get, which was not much. We were in a pretty sorry state, most of us without caps or jackets, and we obtained food from other units that we passed on the road.

We were marching, dismounted, day and night, till we reached the railhead, where I was transferred to the base and sent home. The sergeant-major and Osborne came home at the same time, and the sergeant-major is now a commissioned officer. So is Sergeant Nelson.

After such a furious fight and all the hardships and sufferings of Mons and the retreat, it seems strange and unreal to be back in peaceful London. I don't know what will happen to me, of course, but whatever comes I earnestly hope that some day I shall be able to go back to the little camp where we fought in the morning mist in such a deadly hail of shell, and look at the resting-places of the brave officers and men who gave their lives to save the battery they loved so well.

Battle of Vimy Ridge by Richard Jack - Canadian War Museum

Chapter XI - A Daisy-Chain of Bandoliers

Private W. H. Cooperwaite, Durham Light Infantry.

[In this story we become acquainted with a brilliant bit of work done by our brave little Gurkhas, fresh from India, and we learn of a splendid achievement under a deadly fire—the sort of act for which many of the Victoria Crosses awarded recently have been given. The teller of this story was, at the time of writing, home from the front. He is Private W. H. Cooperwaite, 2nd Battalion Durham Light Infantry, a fine type of the Northerners who have done so much and suffered so heavily in the war.]

I WAS wounded at Ypres—badly bruised in the back by a piece of a "Jack Johnson." There is nothing strange in that, and people have got used to hearing of these German shells; but the main thing about this particular customer was that it was the only one that burst out of eighteen "Jack Johnsons" I counted at one time. If the other seventeen had blown up, I and a lot more of the Durhams would not have been left alive. That same shell killed two of my comrades.

We went into action very soon after leaving England. We had had plenty of tough marching, and on the way we grew accustomed to the terrible evidences of the Germans' outrages.

In one place, going towards Coulommiers, we came across tracks of the German hosts. They had ravaged and destroyed wherever they had passed, and amongst other sights our battalion saw were the bodies of two young girls who had been murdered. The men didn't say much when they set eyes on that, but they marched a good deal quicker, and so far from feeling any fear about meeting the Germans, the sole wish was to get at them.

After a four days' march we got to Coulommiers, where we came up with the French, who had been holding the Germans back and doing fine work. That was in the middle of September, when the Battle of the Aisne was in full swing. On the 19th we went into the trenches, and after a spell in them we were billeted in a house. We had settled down nicely and comfortably, when crash came a shell, and so tremendous was the mischief it did that we had only just time to make a rush and clear out before the house collapsed.

It just sort of fell down, as if it was tired out, and what had been our billet was a gaping ruin. That was the kind of damage which was being done in all directions, and it told with sorry effect on those who were not so lucky as we had been, and were buried in the smash. All the cellars were crowded with people who had taken refuge in them, and they lived in a state of terror and misery during these continuous bombardments by German guns.

After that lively bit of billeting we returned to the trenches, and on Sunday, the 20th, with the West Yorkshires on our right, we were in the very thick of heavy fighting. The artillery on both sides was firing furiously, and the rifles were constantly going. Our own fire from the trenches was doing very heavy mischief amongst the Germans, and they were losing men at such a rate that it was clear to them that they would have to take some means of stopping it, or get so badly mauled that they could not keep the fight going.

Suddenly there was a curious lull in the fighting and we saw that a perfect horde of the Germans were marching up to the West Yorkshires, carrying a huge flag of truce.

It was a welcome sight, and we thought, "Here's a bit of pie for the Tykes—they must have been doing good." They had lost heavily, but it seemed from this signal of surrender that they were to be rewarded for their losses.

A large party of the West Yorkshires went out to meet the Germans with the flag, and I watched them go up until they were within fifty yards of the enemy. I never suspected that anything wrong would happen, nor did the West Yorkshires, for the surrender appeared to be a fair and aboveboard business.

When only that short distance separated the Germans and the West Yorkshires, the leading files of the surrender party fell apart like clockwork and there were revealed to us, behind the flag of truce, stretchers with machine-guns on them, and these guns were set to work at point-blank range on the West Yorkshires, who, utterly surprised and unprepared, were simply mown down, and suffered fearfully before they could pull themselves together.

Now, this dastardly thing was done in full view of us; we could see it all, and our blood just boiled. What we would have liked best of all was a bayonet charge; but the Germans were too far off for the steel, and it seemed as if they were going to have it all their own way.

They had given us a surprise, and a bad one; but we had a worse in store for them—we also had machine-guns, and they were handy, and we got them to work on the dirty tricksters and fairly cut them up. The whole lot seemed to stagger as our bullets showered into them. That was one of the cowardly games the Germans often played at the beginning of the war; but it did not take the British long to get used to them, and very soon the time came when no risks were taken, and the stretcher dodge was played out.

That Sunday brought with it some heavy fighting, and some very sad losses. There was with us an officer whose family name is very particularly associated with the Durham Light Infantry, and that was Major Robb, as good and brave a gentleman as ever breathed.

After that proof of German treachery he received information that the Germans meant to attack us again; but Major Robb thought it would be better to turn things about, and let *us* do the attacking. I dare say he was burning to help to avenge the losses of the West Yorkshires, the poor fellows who were lying dead and wounded all around us.

To carry out an attack like that was a desperate undertaking, because the Germans were six hundred yards away, and the ground was all to their advantage. It rose towards them, and they were on the skyline, so that it became doubly difficult to reach them.

Well, the order was given to advance, and we got out of our trenches and covered most of the distance in good order. Bit by bit we made our way over the rising ground towards that skyline which was a blaze of fire, and from which there came shells and bullets constantly.

There could be no such thing, of course, as a dash, however swift, towards the skyline; we had to creep and crawl and make our way so as to give them as little to hit as possible; but it was terrible—too terrible.

We fell down under that deadly blast, and though I am not a particularly religious man, I'll own that I offered up a prayer, and the man on my left said something of the same sort too. Poor chap! He had scarcely got the words out of his mouth, when over he went, with a bullet in his neck, and there he lay, while those of us who were fit and well kept up and crept up.

At last we were near enough to the skyline to give the Germans rapid fire, and we rattled away as fast as we could load and shoot, till the rifles were hot with firing. After that rapid fire we crept up again, and it was then that I saw Major Robb lying down, facing us, and smoking a pipe—at least he had a pipe in his mouth, just as cool as usual. He sang out to my platoon officer, "How are you feeling, Twist?"

Lieutenant Twist answered, "Oh, I'm about done for." I looked at him and saw that he was wounded in the chest and arm. We had to go on, and we could not take him back just then.

The lieutenant had scarcely finished speaking when I saw Major Robb himself roll over on his side. A poor lad named Armstrong, with four more of our men, crept up to attend to the major, but a piece of shrapnel struck the lad on the head and killed him—and other men were falling all around me.

There was no help for it now—we had to get back to our trenches, if we could; that was our only chance, as the Germans were hopelessly greater in number than we were. So we made our way back as best we could, and we took with us as many of the wounded as we could get hold of.

Time after time our men went back for the wounded; but, in spite of all we could do, some of the wounded had to be left where they had fallen.

We got back, the survivors of us, to the trenches, and we had hardly done so when we heard a shout. We looked up from the trenches, and saw Major Robb on the skyline, crawling a little way.

Instantly a whole lot of us volunteered to go and fetch the major in; but three were picked out—Lance-Corporal Rutherford, Private Warwick, and Private Nevison.

Out from the trenches the three men went; up the rising ground they crawled and crept; then, at the very skyline, Rutherford and Nevison were shot dead, and Warwick was left alone. But he was not left for long. Private Howson went to help him, and he actually got to the ridge and joined him, and the two managed to raise the major up; but as soon as that had been done the officer was shot in a vital part, and Warwick also was hit.

More help went out, and the major and Warwick were brought in; but I grieve to say that the poor major, who was loved by all of us, died soon after he reached the trenches.

That furious fight had cost the Durhams very dearly. When the roll was called we found that we had lost nearly 600 men, and that in my own company only one officer was left. This was Lieutenant Bradford, one of the bravest men I ever saw. At one time, when we had lost a young officer and a man with a machine-gun, Lieutenant Bradford worked the gun himself. I am sorry to say that he was killed in another battle later on.

Now I am going to leave the Valley of the Aisne and get round to Flanders, where we found ourselves near Ypres, faced by a big force of Germans.

Again we were with our friends the West Yorkshires—they were on our right, and on our left we had the East Yorkshires, so that there were three North-country regiments together. Near Ypres we soon had to carry out a smart bit of work which, in a way, proved very pathetic. The Durhams were ordered to take a small village, and we went for it. We reached a farmhouse, and there we found about a score of women and children. Some of our men were sent into the house, but they could not make the women and children understand English. The poor souls were terrified; they had had to do with Germans, and as they were not familiar with our uniforms they thought we were Germans too—another lot of the breed from which they had suffered so much.

We fetched Captain Northey to explain things to the women, and as he entered the house a shell burst near him and took off part of one of his trouser-legs, but without hurting him. The captain took no notice of this little drawback, and into the house he went, and made the women understand that we were English troops; and I can assure you that when they realised that they simply went wild with joy, and hugged and kissed us.

We had gone out to learn, if we could, something about the enemy's strength, and we got to know that there were about 30,000 Germans in front of our brigade, and that they were entrenched.

The Sherwood Foresters, who were in reserve to us, were ordered to relieve us, and it was wonderful to see they way in which they came into the village we had taken, smoking cigarettes as if they were doing a sort of route-march, although they came right up against a hail of bullets, with the usual shells. In face of such tremendous odds they had to retire; but, like good soldiers, they prepared another lot of trenches near the village, and later on we went into them.

In such fighting as this war brings about there are many, many sad incidents, and one of the saddest I know of occurred at this particular village. There was a fine young soldier named Matthews, who came from West Hartlepool, I think it was. He was struck by shrapnel, and we saw that he was badly hurt. We did what we could for him, but it was clear that he was mortally wounded, and that he knew it. His last thought was for home and wife, and he said he would like his cap-badge to be sent to her, to be made into a brooch. I believe that a comrade, who was also a neighbour of his, undertook to do this for him.

It was my good fortune to see the little Gurkhas rout the enemy, who had attacked them, and to give the Germans a most unpleasant shock.

The Germans had been shelling the East Yorkshires, who were now on the right of the Durhams. The enemy had the range almost to an inch, and the effect of the shelling was terrible. Hour after hour this shelling was kept up pitilessly, and the German aeroplanes—"birds," we called them—swooped about and saw the havoc that was being done. This sort of thing went on till after dark, and the Durhams wondered if any of the East Yorkshires were left.

There was a surprise in store for us at dawn next day when we awoke, for the East Yorkshires' trenches were full of Gurkhas, who had slipped in during the night. The Germans knew nothing of this. All they knew was that their shells had been pounding on the East Yorkshires for hours, and doubtless they had satisfied themselves that no troops on earth could stand such a gruelling.

The Germans came on pretty confidently, after dawn, to the position of the East Yorkshires—came on in a cloud. That was after we had repulsed an attack on ourselves, but not finally, owing to the vast numbers of the Germans. Perhaps they expected to find the trenches filled with English dead and wounded, and certainly to us it seemed as if the trenches must be in that condition, for the Gurkhas let the Germans come on without showing a sign of life.

The Germans gave enough warning—as they always do. Bugles sounded, and they rushed on, shouting and yelling; but still there was no sound from the trenches, no sign of life was seen. Even we, who had a fine view of the trenches, could see nothing. We were intensely interested, though we had plenty of hard work to do ourselves in firing at the enemy.

When the Germans got to within about forty yards of the trenches on our left, the little brown fellows, who had been lying so low, sprang up and simply poured over the tops of the trenches. That performance was one of the most extraordinary things seen in the war. The Gurkhas never even attempted to fire; they just seemed to roll over the ground, gripping their long, curved knives.

We were too far off to see exactly what sort of expression came on the Germans' faces when the trenches, which were supposed to be choked with dead and wounded Britons, vomited these Indian warriors; but we saw the whole shouting, yelling line of Germans pull up sharp.

The Germans made a half-hearted effort to come on, then they wavered badly, and well they might, for by this time the little Gurkhas were on them with fury, and the blades flashed like lightning about the mass of startled Germans.

Stunned by the unexpectedness and swiftness of the Indian onslaught, terrified by the deadly wielding of the knives, the Germans made no real effort to withstand the rush from the trenches, and they broke and ran like rabbits, throwing down their rifles as they scuttled, with the Gurkhas leaping after them and doing fearful execution.

It was truly great, and as the victorious little warriors came back we gave them a cheer that was a real hurrah. We were as pleased as the Gurkhas were, and they showed their joy as they came back wiping their knives. They seemed all grin and knife as they returned, and we felt all the better for it, too, especially as we gave the broken, flying Germans a heavy peppering.

Only the Germans who were behind got away, or had a chance. Those in front, who had had to meet the Indians' swift, fierce spring, were done for as soon as the curved blades were whirling amongst them.

I had had a pretty good innings by this time, and had escaped serious injury, but I was very soon to be bowled out. The Durhams were supporting the West Yorkshires, who had been badly cut up. We received word that the West Yorkshires had run short of ammunition, and that fresh supplies were urgently wanted. We advanced with supplies, and found that we had to cover about fifty yards of open ground. The Germans had got the exact range of this open ground, so that it was impossible to advance over it, except singly. The shell and rifle fire was particularly heavy, and it seemed as if nothing could live on that exposed stretch.

One by one we made a dash across that awful space towards the trenches where the Yorkshiremen were hungering for fresh ammunition, and each of us carried a full bandolier for the Tykes. A good many of our men fell, but a lot got through and took part in a very strange bit of work.

I got through myself, after being blown down by the force of a shell explosion near me—thank Heaven it was the force and not the shell itself that knocked me over for the moment! It was terrible going, for we soon found, after we began to make the journey, that we could not quite reach the Yorkshires' trenches.

There were some haystacks on the open ground, and we dodged behind them and dashed from one to the other, every dash meaning a shower of bullets from the Germans.

There was still the last fifty yards I have mentioned to be covered; but now it meant almost sure destruction to be seen, so we threw the bandoliers to the end man in the trenches, the man nearest to us; but a full bandolier is a heavy thing, and there was not much chance of taking aim. We were almost at our wits' end, but we tried another way. We made a sort of daisy-chain of several bandoliers, and paid this out as best we could towards the trenches.

The nearest man in the trench—a plucky chap he was—slipped out and made a dart for the end of the chain. He just made a mad grab and got it. Then he dashed back to his trench, and it seemed as if the business was all over, and that the daisy-chain would be safely hauled in; but to the grief of all of us the chain broke when a few yards of it had been pulled in.

This was a dreadful disappointment, but still something had been done, some rounds of ammunition, at any rate, had been got into the trenches, and we were determined that the Tykes should have some more. We had to wait a bit, for as soon as the Yorkshireman had shot back to his trench, the ground that he had scuttled over was absolutely churned up by shells, and if he had been caught on it he would have been blown to rags. We lost no time in making other efforts, and at last the ammunition was safely delivered to the West Yorkshires in the trenches, and they did some rattling good business with it.

I have mentioned "Jack Johnsons," and I want to speak of them again by way of finish. It was at Ypres that I was bowled out. These "J.J.'s" were falling heavily, but many of them were what you might call dumb—they didn't speak. As I have said, I counted eighteen as they came, and out of the whole of that number only one exploded. But it was enough. I have already told you what happened to two of my comrades, and as for myself it settled me for the time being by badly bruising my spine and back.

And that's the reason why I was invalided home.

A concrete pillbox from World War One - Image: Evelyn Simak

Chapter XII – Despatch-Riding

Corporal Hedley G. Browne, Royal Engineers.

[Particularly hard and responsible work has been done for the British Army by motor cycle despatch-riders. Many members of this fine branch of our fighting men abandoned very promising careers in civil life to go to the seat of war. Amongst them is Corporal Hedley G. Browne, Captain of the Norfolk Motor Cycle Club, who when war broke out volunteered for active service and became a motor cycle despatch-rider, attached to a signal company of the Royal Engineers. It is his story which is here retold. Of the work of the motor cycle despatch-riders Sir John French has spoken in terms of high praise, and when the King visited the front recently a number of the riders were specially brought to his Majesty's notice.]

I WAS in Ypres, billeted in a brewery, when that beautiful old city was still intact; I was there when the first German shell came and began the ruthless bombardment which has laid the city in ruins and added one more to the list of heavy debts which the Germans will have to pay when the war is over. The sooner that time comes the better, especially for those who have been at the front since the beginning, and have had to endure things which people at home cannot possibly realise. Five days ago I left the front for a flying visit home, and now I am on my way back. It has seemed a very short spell, and a big slice of the time has been eaten up in travelling. A nice batch of us came over together, and here we are assembling again, though it's a good hour before the boat-train starts.

We go to Boulogne, and then we shall get into motor lorries and be trundled off back to the fighting line. This is the kit we work and live in—even now my revolver is loaded in every chamber. No, so far, I haven't used it on a German; but it's shot a pig or two when we've wanted pork, and really there isn't much difference between the two. It is hard to believe that human beings committed some of the acts of which I saw so many during those four months at the front. The astounding thing is that the Germans don't realise that they have done anything wrong, and quite lately I was talking with some German prisoners who spoke English, who not only did not see this, but were also quite sure that the war will end in favour of Germany. By this time, however, they are changing their tune.

When I got to the front I was attached to a signal company, which consists of establishing communication between headquarters and three brigades, and that meant when we were on the march riding through about seven miles of troops, guns, waggons and hosts of other things. When in action we had to go quite up to the firing line, and very soon I hardly knew myself, as I got quite used to the bursting of shells and to the shocking condition of the killed and wounded. It was astonishing to see how soon men, who had been used to every comfort at home and who knew nothing of war in any shape or form, got accustomed to the hardships of campaigning and developed a callousness which is altogether foreign to their real nature.

One of the most amazing things about the war is the way in which it changes a man and makes him callous. I know that before I had anything to do with the Army I was so sensitive in some ways that the mere thought of blood was almost enough to make me ill, yet now, after being for more than four months in the war, and having seen the havoc of the most terrific battles the world has ever known, I tear along the lonely roads and remain almost unmoved by the most dreadful sights. The dead pass unnoticed, and as for the wounded, you can do nothing, as a rule. You have your orders, and they must be obeyed without loss of time, because a motor despatch-rider is always on the rush.

I well remember the very first German I saw lying dead. He was an Uhlan, and was on the roadside. I was greatly distressed at the sight of him, there was something so sad about it all, but now there is no such sensation at the sight of even great numbers of the dead. A strange thing happened in connection with the Uhlan. I took his cap as a memento, and brought it home, with several other German caps and helmets, chunks of shell, clips of cartridges, and relics of altar-cloths; and now, for some cause which I can't quite fathom, the Uhlan's cap has turned a queer sort of yellow.

That strange callousness comes over one at the most unexpected times, and often enough a motor despatch-rider has to dash through a crowd of refugees and scatter them, though the very sight of the poor souls is heartbreaking. When Ypres was bombarded, the men, women and children thronged the roads, and all that was left to them in the world they carried in bundles on their backs; yet they had to be scattered like flocks of sheep when the motor despatch-riders rushed along. There was, however, one pleasing feature in the matter, and that was that these poor people knew that we were tearing along in their interests as well as our own, and that we did not mean to hurt anybody—which was different, indeed, from the spirit of the enemy, whose policy was to spread terror and havoc wherever he could, and to destroy mercilessly. When I first went into Ypres it was a beautiful old city, very much like Norwich, but I saw the German guns smash the place and the shells set fire to glorious old structures like the Cathedral and the Cloth Hall. The two pieces of altar-cloth which I brought home were taken from the Cathedral while it was burning.

Though you soon get used to war, still there are always things coming along which are either particularly interesting or very thrilling. Perhaps the most exciting incident I can call to mind is the bringing down of a German aeroplane by a British brigade. That was on October 27th, when I was with the brigade. It was afternoon, and the aeroplane was flying fairly low, so that it was a good target for the rain of bullets which was directed on it. Even when flying low, an aeroplane is not easy to hit, because of its quick, dodging movements, but this machine was fairly got by the brigade. Suddenly there was an explosion in the aeroplane, flames shot out and the machine made a sickening, terrible somersault. I took it that a bullet or two had struck the petrol tank and blown the machine up—anyway, the airman was shot out and crashed to earth with fearful speed. You wanted to look away, but an awful fascination made you keep your eyes on what was happening. At first the man looked like a piece of paper coming down, then, almost before you could realise the tragedy that was taking place, the piece of paper took the form of a fellow-creature—then the end came. The man himself smashed to earth about two hundred yards from the spot where I was watching, but the machine dropped some distance off. That was really one of the sights that no amount of war will accustom you to, and I shall never forget it as long as I live.

At first the weather was very hot, which made the work for the troops very hard. The machine I had soon struck work, and was left to be handed over to the Kaiser as a souvenir; and several other machines gave up the ghost in like manner. When a machine went wrong, it was left and a new one took its place—the list of casualties for motors of every sort is an amazingly heavy one; but casualties were inevitable, because in many places the roads that we had to take were perfect nightmares.

It was very hard going till we got used to it. During the first month at the front I had my boots off about three times—I am now wearing my fourth pair, which is an average of one a month—and we reckoned that we were lucky if we slept in a barn, with straw; if we couldn't manage that we turned in anywhere, in our greatcoats. When I say sleep, I mean lying down for an hour or two, as sometimes we did not billet till dark. Then we had some grub, anything we could get, and after that a message. Next day we were off, five times out of six, at 3.30 to four o'clock, and got long, hard days in.

Amongst the messages we had to carry there were none more urgent than those which were sent for reinforcements, the men upon whose coming the issue of a battle depended. It was tear and scurry all along, but somehow the message would get delivered all right and the reinforcements would hurry up and save the situation. Often enough a message would be delivered at midnight to a tired officer who was living in a dug-out, and I scarcely ever reached one of these warrens without being invited to take something of whatever was going—it might be a drink of hot coffee, with a biscuit, or a tot of rum, which was truly grateful after a bitter ride. That is the only thing in the way of alcoholic drink at the front, and very little of it. This is, for the British, a teetotal war; but for the Germans it has been the very reverse, and time after time we came across evidence of their drunken debauches.

The shell fire was so incessant that it was soon taken as part of the day's work. At first it was terrible, though one got used to it. My first experience of rifle fire did not come until I had been at the front for some weeks, and then I was surprised to find what a comparatively small thing it is compared with shells—it is not nearly so bad.

It was getting dark, and it was my duty to go down a lane where snipers were hidden in the trees. This was just the kind of lane you know in England, and you can easily picture what it meant. Imagine leaving your machine, as I did, in a tree-lined lane at home, and going down it, knowing that there were fellows up the trees who were on the watch to pot you, and you will realise what it meant; but you will have to picture also the sides of the lane being littered, as this was, with dead and wounded men. Well, I had to go down that lane, and I went—sometimes walking, sometimes running, with the bullets whizzing round and the shells bursting. But by good luck I escaped the bullets, though a piece of shell nearly nailed me—or would have got me if I had been with my machine. The fragment struck the cycle and I picked it up and brought it home with the other things as a souvenir.

That escape was practically nothing. It was a detail, and came in the day's work; but I had a much more narrow shave a few days later. It was a Saturday and I had had a pretty hard time—amongst other things I had done a thirty-mile ride after one o'clock in the morning—the sort of ride that takes it out of you.

There was one of our orderlies with a horse near me and I was standing talking to him. We heard a shrapnel shell coming, and ducked our heads instinctively to dodge it—but the shell got at us. The horse was killed and the orderly was so badly hit that he died in less than an hour. He was buried in the afternoon, and very solemn the funeral was, with the guns booming all around. I was deeply shocked at the time, but war is war, and in a very short time the incident had passed out of my mind. Our fellows told me that I was one of the lucky ones that day.

That was the beginning of one of the most awful periods of the war, especially for the despatch-riders, for we were at it night and day. The roads were hopelessly bad, and as we were not allowed to carry any lamps at night the danger of rapid travel was greatly increased. We were, however, relieved to some extent by mounted men. The fighting was furious and incessant, and we were in the thick of a good deal of it. After a very hard spell I was quartered all day in a little stable, and it proved to be about the most dangerous place I had come across. On October 29th the Germans went for the stable with high explosives and the everlasting "scuttles." For some time these big shells came and burst in the locality, and two houses within a score of yards of us were blown to pieces and enormous holes were driven in the ground.

From the stable we went to a house, and then we fairly got it. Four huge shells came, one after the other, and one came and ripped the roof just like paper. We were amazingly lucky, however, for the worst thing that happened was that a fellow was wounded in the leg. I was thankful when the order came to pack up and stand by, for there were in that little place about twenty of us from different regiments, and a single explosion would have put us all well beyond the power of carrying either despatches or anything else. For a while we could not understand why the enemy should so greatly favour us, but we soon learned that they were going for some French guns near us. So the firing went on, and when we went to sleep, as we did in spite of all, bullets ripped through the roof, coming in at one side of the building and going out at the other, and four more big shells paid us a most unwelcome visit.

I was thankful when we moved out of those unpleasant quarters and took up our abode in a large farmhouse about three hundred yards away. This was one of the very few buildings that had escaped the ravages of the German artillery fire. We made the move on the 30th, when the cannonade was very heavy, yet the only casualties were a pig and two horses. We were now much better protected from the Germans' fire, though the very house shook with the artillery duel and the noise grew deafening and almost maddening. I wrote home pretty often, and I remember that at this time I got behind a hedge to write a letter, and as I wrote bullets whizzed over my head, fired by German snipers who were up some trees not very far away. They were going for our chaps in the trenches a mile away.

Mons had been bad, and there had been many harrowing sights on the retreat, but at the end of October and the beginning of November the climax of horror was reached. The Germans, mad to hack their way through to the coast, and perhaps realising that they would never do it, stuck at nothing. They were frantic, and I saw sights that would sicken any human being. No consideration weighed with them, they simply did their best to annihilate us—but they are trying still to do that and not succeeding.

We had left the farmhouse and gone into a large château, which served as headquarters, and here, on November 2nd, we had a ghastly experience. It is likely that the Germans knew the particular purpose to which the château had been devoted; at any rate they shelled it mercilessly, and no fewer than six staff officers were killed, while a considerable number were wounded. Again I was lucky, and came out of the adventure unscathed. On the following day, however, I was nearly caught. I had taken a message to headquarters and was putting my machine on a stand. To do this I had to leave a house, and go about fifty yards away, to the stand. I had scarcely left the building when two shells struck it fair and plump, and killed two motor cyclists and wounded three others. Like a flash I jumped into a ditch, and as I did so I heard the bits of burst shell falling all around me. When I got out of the ditch and went back along the main road I saw a huge hole which a shell had made. It was a thrilling enough escape, and shook me at the time, because I knew the two poor fellows who were killed. That was the kind of thing we went through as we jogged along from day to day.

I am not, of course, giving a story of the war so much as trying to show what it means to be a motor cycle despatch-rider at the front. He is here, there and everywhere—and there is no speed limit. He is not in the actual firing line, yet he sees a great deal of what is going on. Sometimes he is very lucky, as I was myself one day, in being allowed to witness a fight that was taking place. I had taken a despatch to an officer, and perhaps conveyed some cheering news. Anyway, I had the chance to go to an eminence from which I could view the battle, and I went, and it was wonderful to see the waging of the contest over a vast tract of country—for in a war like this the ordinary fighter sees very little indeed of the battle. At this special point I had the rare chance of witnessing a fight as I suppose it is seen by the headquarters staff, and one of the strangest things about it was the little there was to be seen. There were puffs of smoke and tongues of flame—and the everlasting boom of guns; but not much more. Men are killed at long distances and out of sight in these days.

War is excessively wearing, and it was a blessed relief when a day came which was free from shells and bullets. That, indeed, was the calm after the storm. It came to us when we were snug in a farmyard about a mile away from a big town, with our motor-cars, cycles and horses so well under cover that the German aeroplanes did not find us out. Thankful indeed were we for the change, because the whole region where we were had been pitilessly bombarded, and there was nothing but devastation around us. Shells had done their work, and there was a special kind of bomb which fired anything it touched that was inflammable. A great many petrol discs, about the size of a shilling, were discharged by the Germans, and these things, once alight, did amazing mischief. Villages were obliterated, and in the big town where we were billeted the engineers were forced to blow up the surrounding houses to prevent the entire place from being destroyed.

The glad time came when our Division was relieved for a time. We got a bit of rest, and I crossed the Channel and came home for a short spell. One of the last things I saw before I left the front was the Prince of Wales making a tour. At that time he was about fifteen miles from the firing line.

What was the most noticeable thing that struck me when I came back over the Channel? Well, that is not easy to say, but I know that I particularly noticed the darkness of the London streets.

"The men were told to lay hands on anything that would float."

Printed in Great Britain
by Amazon